*R*ECONFIGURING
*F*OOTPRINT
TO SPEED
EXPEDITIONARY AEROSPACE
FORCES DEPLOYMENT

Lionel A. Galway
Mahyar A. Amouzegar
Richard J. Hillestad
Don Snyder

Prepared for the United States Air Force

RAND
Project AIR FORCE

The research reported here was sponsored by the United States Air Force under Contract F49642-01-C-0003. Further information may be obtained from the Strategic Planning Division, Directorate of Plans, Hq USAF.

Library of Congress Cataloging-in-Publication Data

Reconfiguring footprint to speed expeditionary aerospace forces deployment / Lionel A. Galway [et al.].
    p. cm.
    "MR-1625."
    ISBN 0-8330-3298-4 (pbk.)
    1. United States. Air Force—Supplies and stores. 2. Deployment (Strategy) 3. Airlift, Military—United States. 4. United States. Air Force—Reorganization. I. Galway, Lionel A., 1950–

UG1103 .R43 2002
358.4'14—dc21

2002152923

Cover photos courtesy of U.S. Air Force at www.af.mil/photos.
Photographers: Senior Airman Stan Parker, Senior Airman Delia A. Castillo and Staff Sgt. Krista M. Foeller

RAND is a nonprofit institution that helps improve policy and decisionmaking through research and analysis. RAND® is a registered trademark. RAND's publications do not necessarily reflect the opinions or policies of its research sponsors.

Cover design by Barbara Angell Caslon

Published 2002 by RAND
1700 Main Street, P.O. Box 2138, Santa Monica, CA 90407-2138
1200 South Hayes Street, Arlington, VA 22202-5050
201 North Craig Street, Suite 202, Pittsburgh, PA 15213-1516
RAND URL: http://www.rand.org/
To order RAND documents or to obtain additional information, contact Distribution Services: Telephone: (310) 451-7002;
Fax: (310) 451-6915; Email: order@rand.org

This report documents research undertaken in support of emerging Air Force employment strategies associated with Expeditionary Aerospace Forces (EAFs). EAF concepts turn on the premise that highly effective air and space force packages that can be rapidly tailored, quickly deployed, and immediately employed can serve as a credible substitute for permanent forward presence. Success of the EAF will, to a great extent, depend on the effectiveness and efficiency of the Agile Combat Support system, a core competency of the Air Force. Agile Combat Support focuses on speeding the deployment and easing the sustainment of combat forces by reengineering support through improvements in responsiveness, agility, deployability, and sustainability.

This report documents our work on restructuring deployment footprint. One major obstacle in implementing the EAF is the difficulty of deploying support infrastructure that was designed for the Cold War. USAF experience in Desert Storm and Kosovo has led to calls for "footprint reduction" to speed deployment. We argue here that physical reduction of support processes is only one strategy in speeding deployment, and we develop a framework and propose tools that broaden the definition of footprint to allow the integration of several effective strategies. The research addressed in this report was conducted in the Resource Management Program of Project AIR FORCE as the project "Combat Support for Implementing the EAF: Footprint Reduction Definition, Measurement, and Options." The project was sponsored by the Air Force Deputy Chief of Staff for Installations and Logistics (AF/IL) and the Deputy Chief of Staff for Operations (AF/XO). This report should be of interest to logisticians and operators in the Air Force concerned with implementing the EAF concept. This research project was completed in October 2001.

PROJECT AIR FORCE

Project AIR FORCE, a division of RAND, is the Air Force federally funded research and development center (FFRDC) for studies and analyses. It provides the Air Force with independent analyses of policy alternatives affecting the development, employment, combat readiness, and support of current and future aerospace forces. Research is performed in four programs: Aerospace Force Development; Manpower, Personnel, and Training; Resource Management; and Strategy and Doctrine.

CONTENTS

Preface   iii

Figures   vii

Tables   ix

Summary   xi

Acknowledgments   xvii

Acronyms   xix

Chapter One
EXPEDITIONARY AEROSPACE FORCE DEPLOYMENT
AND FOOTPRINT   1
The Expeditionary Aerospace Force   1
Deploying and Supporting the EAF   2
Project Overview   5

Chapter Two
FOOTPRINT: FROM THE COLD WAR TO THE EAF   7
Footprint Hierarchy   8
    UTC Level   9
    Force/Base Level   11
    Theater Level   12
Focus on Force/Base   12
Needed: UTC Lists for Force/Base Packages   14
Examples of Functional Area Footprint Reduction   17
    Methodology   17
    Bare Base Support   18
    Munitions   21

Civil Engineering   22
Vehicles   26
Medical   26
Measuring Footprint Reduction   27

Chapter Three
BEYOND FOOTPRINT: FOOTPRINT
CONFIGURATION   31
Back to the Goal: Time to Combat Capability   31
Parameterized UTC Lists   32
Footprint Configuration   33
   Forward Operating Location versus Remote Support
      Processes   34
   The FOL Segment   35
   The Remote Segment   36
   Putting It All Together: Footprint Configuration   37
Metrics for Evaluating Footprint Configurations   39

Chapter Four
DEVELOPING, EVALUATING, AND TRACKING
ALTERNATIVE FOOTPRINT CONFIGURATIONS   43
Tools for Reconfiguring Footprint   43
Evaluating and Tracking Force/Base Packages   44
   Evaluation   45
   Tracking   48
Evaluating and Tracking Individual UTCs   50
Evaluating and Tracking Theater Footprint
   Configuration   51
Summary   53

Chapter Five
CONCLUSIONS AND RECOMMENDATIONS   55

Bibliography   61

S.1. Schematic Force/Base Footprint Configuration   xiv
1.1. Support Footprint for Aerospace Power Is
      Substantial   3
2.1. Footprint Hierarchy Schematic   9
2.2. Comparison of Selected Planning Footprints 16
2.3. Comparison of Harvest Falcon UTCs, 1996 and
      2001 19
2.4. Comparison of Munitions UTCs, 1996 and 2001 21
2.5. Comparison of Short Tons Required for CE Bare Base
      Deployment, 1996 and 2001 24
2.6. Comparison of Personnel Required for CE Bare Base
      Deployment, 1996 and 2001 25
2.7. Comparison of Four Major Footprint Components,
      1996 and 2001 28
2.8. Comparison of UTCs, 1996 and 2001 29
3.1. Division of Footprint into FOL and Remote Pieces . . . 34
3.2.   Subdivision of FOL Footprint Portion into IOR, FOR,
      and On-Call 35
3.3. Subdivision of Remote Footprint Portion into
      Portions at Forward and CONUS Support Locations . . 36
3.4. Footprint Configuration for a Notional Individual
      Support Process 37
3.5. Combining Footprint Configurations for Multiple
      Support Processes 38
4.1. Model Process to Develop UTC Lists for Specific
      Scenarios and FOL Characteristics 46
4.2. Evaluation Tool for Force/Base Package 47

TABLES

2.1. E-Falcon Component Weights 20
4.1. Tabular Tracking of Force/Base Package (Notional) . . 49
4.2. Tracking Theater Footprint Configuration
      (Notional) 52

EAF DEPLOYMENT AND FOOTPRINT

Since the end of the Cold War, the U.S. Air Force has frequently been deployed overseas, often on short notice, in support of crises ranging from humanitarian relief to Operation Desert Storm. To meet these challenges, the Air Force has implemented a new operational concept, that of the Expeditionary Aerospace Force (EAF), which replaces the permanent forward presence of airpower with a force that can deploy quickly from the continental United States (CONUS) to Forward Operating Locations (FOLs) in response to a crisis, commence operations immediately on arrival, and sustain those operations as needed. In the words of *Air Force Vision 2020*, "We will be able to deploy . . . in 48 hours, fast enough to curb many crises before they escalate."[1]

However, quickly deploying the support structure for aerospace operations is not easy: The consensus of most studies is that moving the support for a force package to an FOL with minimal infrastructure within the notional time frame of 48 hours is almost certainly infeasible given current support process organization and equipment. The equipment and people required to support a combat deployment is simply very heavy. One primary result has been a call for "footprint reduction," i.e., physically reducing the amount of materiel and personnel actually deployed to FOLs. However, for many areas such as munitions, significant mass reduction will require sub-

---

[1]U.S. Air Force, 2001.

stantial investment in new technology and development: replacing a 2000-lb bomb with a smaller munition may require more sophisticated guidance, new explosives with more power, and other modifications such as new techniques for penetration. Results from this investment will take substantial time to mature and can be technically risky. But with a broader definition of footprint, other strategies are available, including time-phasing of support and remote support for certain processes. The objectives of this study were to define footprint, to establish a baseline and metrics whereby progress at reducing footprint could be monitored, and to develop an analysis framework for complementary strategies for speeding deployment under the EAF concept.

FOOTPRINT: FROM THE COLD WAR TO THE EAF

With the advent of the EAF concept, the USAF can no longer assume that most deployments will be to fully equipped active ("warm") bases. For deployments to austere bases, all the materiel and personnel to commence and sustain operations—the deployment "footprint"—must be provided for, whether it is moved in or prepositioned. It is useful to distinguish three levels of footprint: the individual support processes, the complete package needed for a specific force/base combination, and the package needed for a theater composed of multiple forces bedded down at multiple bases. It is a central thesis of this report that the keystone to reducing time to deployment lies in defining requirements at the force/base level and then looking at a wide variety of strategies to cut that time, including not only physical reductions in materiel, but also various forms of centralized theater support.

We therefore need a set of force/base support lists for selected forces and base types. However, *generic* lists (as opposed to historical lists from recent conflicts or from current warplans) are not currently maintained by the Air Force and in their absence it is virtually impossible to track reduction. However, by focusing on five of the heaviest support processes (bare base housekeeping support, munitions, civil engineering, vehicles, and medical), it is possible to see how these have changed since the inception of the EAF concept in 1997. Judging by available data, there has been little *physical* reduction in these areas. This is due partially to the characteristics of the processes: Munitions and earth-moving equipment are intrinsically heavy and have not changed over those five years. Another issue in civil engineering is that firefighting standards became more stringent in 2001, requiring more equipment and firefighters. There were also some egregious data errors relating to the bare base housekeeping equipment. But the most notable insight is that the different areas have worked to reduce their footprint fairly independently, with allocation of resources dictated not by the goal of reducing deployment time over the entire base but by physical reduction only within an area, leading to suboptimization and sometimes conflict between the actions taken by different areas.

BEYOND FOOTPRINT: FOOTPRINT CONFIGURATION

Many functional areas, facing severe technical obstacles to near-term footprint reduction, instead began developing other strategies to speed deployment such as time-phasing support. Others provided support from centralized Forward Support Locations (FSLs) or did not deploy some capabilities unless they were specifically called for.

To evaluate these strategies in a coherent fashion, we developed the concept of *footprint configuration*, in which the materiel and personnel required for any support process is divided into five parts:

- Initial Operating Requirement (IOR): Needed at the FOL to initiate operations (give the base initial operating capability or IOC).

- Full Operating Requirement (FOR): Needed at the FOL to sustain operations and to bring the base to full operating capability or FOC.

- On-call: Needed at the FOL, but only in specific circumstances.

- FSL: Need not be at the FOL. Can be provided at FSLs elsewhere in theater.

- CONUS Support Location (CSL): Need not be at the FOL or in theater, but can be provided from the CONUS.

We expect that different support processes have different subdivisions as shown in Figure S.1. Some may need to be entirely at the FOL, with no part even on-call (e.g., notional support process B).

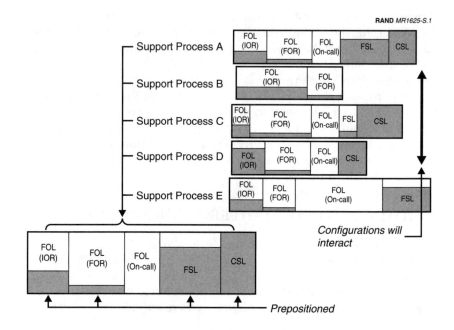

Figure S.1—Schematic Force/Base Footprint Configuration

Others may not have any part at a CSL (process E); in others, the proportion in each segment may vary, along with what can be prepositioned (shaded areas). In contrast, the traditional (and somewhat limited) view of footprint merely considers materiel initially deployed to an FOL.

One advantage of the traditional concept of footprint was that its measurement was conceptually simple: mass of materiel and number of people to be moved. The characteristics of footprint configuration are multidimensional. There are four primary metrics:

- Time to IOC.

- Time to FOC.

- Transportation resources required to move IOR.

- Transportation resources required to move FOR.

Achieving desired values on these four metrics requires trading off and controlling several other key metrics: materiel mass and personnel, cost (investment and recurring), flexibility, risk, and the effect of reconfiguring on the current force.

DEVELOPING, EVALUATING, AND TRACKING ALTERNATIVE FOOTPRINT CONFIGURATIONS

To implement the reconfiguration of footprint, two related types of tools are required:

- *Evaluation tools* to help make strategic support decisions.

- *Tracking tools* to follow the progress in attaining expeditionary deployment goals for specific force/base combinations, key support processes, and theater warplans.

The first requirement for evaluating force/base packages is the ability to assemble the list of Unit Type Codes (UTCs, the basic deployment unit for the Department of Defense (DoD)) that need to be deployed to the base to support the force to be bedded down. Building on these data, an evaluation tool can allow decisionmakers to modify UTCs to allow pieces to be time-phased, prepositioned, or deployed to an FSL instead of to FOLs, with corresponding changes to the different metrics. Once specific footprint configuration decisions have been made, tracking progress at the force/base level can be done by organizing the options into a scorecard type of display that shows how they "score" on many of the metrics as implementation proceeds.

Which force/base packages need to be tracked? For the near future, the warm base type of infrastructure will continue to be important, as will the international airport base infrastructure where warm bases are not prepared. For fighter packages, current planning suggests that the following force packages are the most important: single MDS (mission design series) squadrons, the "canonical" Aerospace Expeditionary Task Force or ASETF (12 each F-15Es, F-15Cs, and F-16CJs) and six-ship, single MDS packages for dispersed operations.

Tracking individual UTCs will be diagnostic in purpose, to help identify promising areas of attack for improving the performance at the force/base level. At the other end of the hierarchy, operational commanders and support planners at the theater level are interested in the deployment and beddown of a large force at multiple sites throughout a theater. Evaluating and tracking the theater-level performance of footprint configurations is then a matter of aggregating performance at individual bases, taking into account the effects of FSLs and CSLs.

CONCLUSIONS AND RECOMMENDATIONS

Using only the strategy of raw footprint reduction to reduce deployment times forgoes the advantages to be had by using multiple strategies of footprint reconfiguration (which include physical reduction). We therefore recommend that the Air Force:

- Develop a comprehensive, parameterized list of UTCs needed to deploy a given force capability to a base with a specified infrastructure. Use actual exercises and deployments to help evaluate these lists.

- Adopt *footprint configuration* as an organizing principle for restructuring support processes.

- Exercise more centralized control of UTC development to ensure that there is a system view taken of UTC modifications.

- Track changes in deployment speed and other major metrics for selected force packages/base infrastructure combinations to evaluate progress.

- Set up a system to aggregate the force/base evaluations to theater level for current warplans and for strategic support planning for proposed plans.

- Develop tools to help decisionmakers evaluate and select among alternative footprint configurations.

ACKNOWLEDGMENTS

Because this project was sponsored by both AF/IL and AF/XO, we required support from the staffs of both organizations. We are grateful to Susan O'Neal (AF/ILX) and Maj Gen Jeffrey Kohler (AF/XOX), who, with their staffs, provided us with contacts and data from very diverse parts of the Air Force. (ILX was eliminated in the 2002 Air Staff reorganization.)

In IL, our primary contacts for information were Col Rodney Boatwright and Col Lori Hill (previous and current ILXX) and their staff: Lt Col Frank Gorman, Lt Col Robert Cleary, David Jacobs, Richard Olsen (ANSER), and MSgt Larry Leach. We benefited from discussions on civil engineering with personnel from AF/ILEX: Col Timothy Byers, Donald Seward, and particularly Joe Smith at the Air Force Civil Engineering Support Agency. At AF/ILMW, Lt Col Eric Gates, CMSgt Phillip Kennedy, and CMSgt James Crum provided us with information on munitions support. We had other helpful discussions with Lt Col Rick Jones (AF/ILMY), Maj John Anderson (AF/ILTR), James Halvorson (AF/ILV), and Lt Col Sean Cassidy (AF/ILXS). Concurrent with our study, Synergy, Inc., was developing a roadmap for footprint reduction under contract to ILX, and we had several informative discussions with Donald Zimmerman, Carey Burke, Michael Golson, and David Barrett of Synergy.

We want to thank especially Lt Col Greg Schwab (XOX) for his tireless efforts to help us find data and to get access to people. We also received significant help from Col Steven Cullen (AF/XOX), Gail Halloran (AF/XOXW), and Col Roberts, Lt Col Jack Smith, and Col Dale Hewitt (AF/XOFP). Other Air Staff informants were Lt Col Larry May and Maj Doreen Pagel (AF/SGXR). We thank Maj William Scott (AF/SAA) for sharing his briefing and data on Operation Noble Anvil. At the Air Force's Logistics Management Agency, we obtained valuable information and advice from Capt Timothy Gillaspie and SMSgt Cedric McMillan.

At the MAJCOMs and units, we talked with Pete Clements (ACC/LGXW), Lt Col William Doneth (CENTAF/DOXL), Walt Franklin at the AEF Center, Maj David Belz (USAFE/LSS/CC), Lt Col Larry Hudson (USAFE/LGX), Col Russell Grunch (607 ASG/CC), Col David Smith and Sgt John McNulty (PACAF/LGX), Col James Lyons and Capt Paul Smith (49 MMG/CC and 49MMG/LGX), Capt Scott Hall and his colleagues (366WG/LGX), and Maj Christopher Ferrez (1FW/LGLX).

As always, we received data, advice, and counsel from a wide variety of RAND colleagues, including (in alphabetical order): Kip Miller, C. Robert Roll, Hyman Shulman, and Robert Tripp. Robert Mullins, who was in AF/XOX during the period when this research was conducted, was especially helpful. We also benefited from careful reviews by Carl Rhodes and Robert Wolff.

As always, the analysis and conclusions are the responsibility of the authors.

ACRONYMS

ACC	Air Combat Command
AEF	Aerospace Expeditionary Force
AEW	Air Expeditionary Wing
AF	Air Force
AFB	Air Force Base
AMRAAM	Advanced Medium-Range Air-to-Air Missile
ASETF	Aerospace Expeditionary Task Force
ATH	Air Transportable Hospital
CE	Civil Engineering/Engineers
CENTAF	Central Air Forces
CIRF	Centralized Intermediate Repair Facility
CONUS	Continental United States
CORONA	Meeting of USAF Generals to discuss key corporate policy issues
CSL	CONUS Support Location
DoD	Department of Defense
EAF	Expeditionary Aerospace Force

ECU	Environmental Control Unit
EMEDS	Expeditionary Medical Support
EOD	Explosive Ordnance Disposal
FAM	Functional Area Manager
FOC	Full Operating Capability
FOL	Forward Operating Location
FOR	Full Operating Requirement
FSL	Forward Support Location
FW	Fighter Wing
GBU	Guided Bomb Unit
IOC	Initial Operating Capability
IOR	Initial Operating Requirement
JEIM	Jet Engine Intermediate Maintenance
LANTIRN	Low-Altitude Navigation and Targeting Infrared for Night
LGX	Logistics Plans
LRU	Line Replaceable Unit
MAJCOM	Major Command
MDS	Mission Design Series
MEFPAK	Manpower and Equipment Force Packaging
MISCAP	Mission Capability
MMG	Materiel Management Group
MTW	Major Theater War
NBC	Nuclear, Biological, and Chemical

ONA	Operation Noble Anvil
PAA	Primary Aircraft Authorized
PACAF	Pacific Air Forces
PAX	Passengers
Prime BEEF	Prime Base Engineer Emergency Force
RED HORSE	Rapid Engineer Deployable Heavy Operations Repair Squadron Engineer
RSC	Regional Support Center
RSS	Regional Supply Squadron
SAA	Studies and Analysis
SDB	Small Diameter Bomb
SEAD	Suppression of Enemy Air Defenses
SSC	Small Scale Contingency
TPFDD	Time-Phased Force Deployment Data
USAF	U.S. Air Force
USAFE	U.S. Air Forces Europe
UTC	Unit Type Code
WRM	War Reserve Materiel

Chapter One

EXPEDITIONARY AEROSPACE FORCE DEPLOYMENT AND FOOTPRINT

THE EXPEDITIONARY AEROSPACE FORCE

Since the end of the Cold War, the United States has found itself in a new and continually changing security environment: Instead of facing a known enemy in a limited number of locations (Europe and Korea), the U.S. military has frequently been deployed overseas, often on short notice, in support of crises ranging in size from humanitarian relief to Operation Desert Storm. This pattern of fast-breaking, varied regional crises and rapid, far-flung deployments appears to be the model for the foreseeable future as is evident in our involvement in Afghanistan. The U.S. Air Force (USAF) has been and will continue to be heavily involved in all of these operations.

The new environment has put a substantial burden on Air Force personnel and equipment.[1] Even in situations that required only land-based airpower for deterrence, the only option has been to deploy aircraft, personnel, and support equipment to the theater of operations and to keep them there. To ease that burden, the Air Force has reorganized into an Expeditionary Aerospace Force (EAF). The aim of that reorganization is to replace the forward presence of airpower with a force that can deploy quickly from the continental United States (CONUS) in response to a crisis, commence operations im-

---

[1] For example, in fiscal year 1999, USAF operations included 38,000 sorties associated with Allied Force, 19,000 sorties to enforce the no-fly zones in Iraq, and about 70,000 mobility missions to more than 140 countries (Sweetman, 2000).

mediately upon arrival, and sustain those operations as needed. In implementing the EAF, the Air Force has divided its forces into roughly ten Aerospace Expeditionary Forces (AEFs), each with a mix of fighters, bombers, and tankers, and keeps two AEFs on-call for 90-day periods to handle crises, leaving 12 months between on-call periods for each AEF.[2] In the words of *Air Force Vision 2020*, "We will be able to deploy an AEF in 48 hours, fast enough to curb many crises before they escalate."[3]

DEPLOYING AND SUPPORTING THE EAF

One key question in implementing the EAF is whether the Air Force can deploy a capable aerospace force in a very short time and have it immediately begin and sustain operations. Given the current structure of the force, with its predominance of relatively short-range fighter aircraft, employment requires operation from Forward Operating Locations (FOLs) in theater within a few hundred miles of potential targets if high sortie rates are to be maintained.[4] Bombers can operate from CONUS (and did so in the Kosovo operations) but, again, maintaining a high sortie rate requires ground support that must be located near the area of operations.

Clearly, if the on-call AEF has aircraft and crews ready on short notice, a 48-hour deployment of the combat aircraft themselves is feasible in terms of raw flying time. However, quickly deploying the support structure for fighter movement and operations is not as easy. We will be concerned here with assembling and moving the necessary support structure (equipment and personnel) to the FOL (and in fact defining just what is necessary). We note that organizing airlift and other transportation to accomplish the deployment, and building and maintaining the "tanker bridge" to support both combat air-

---

[2]Currently, two "pop-up" forces alternate alert duties for quick reaction. One is the 366th Wing at Mountain Home Air Force Base (AFB), the lead wing for the other is the 4th Fighter Wing (FW) at Seymour Johnson AFB.

[3]The on-call AEFs provide the forces and personnel to staff current rotations such as Northern and Southern Watch on the same 90-day cycle. This arrangement should greatly reduce current personnel turbulence, which has been linked by some to recent decreases in both retention and readiness. (See U.S. Air Force, 2001.)

[4]Obviously, fighters can be refueled for longer missions, but at the cost of additional complexity in mission planning and a reduction in sortie rates.

craft and transport airlift, are also nontrivial support tasks, but the first step is clearly to determine what needs to be moved. The support processes, in fact, constitute the major portion of any deployment (see Figure 1.1 for an example of 4th Aerospace Expeditionary Wing (AEW) deployment in early 1997).[5]

Given that most of the current combat platforms and their support systems were designed for operations central to Cold War strategy (i.e., to fly largely from prepared bases with prepositioned equipment), it is not surprising that little of the support equipment was explicitly designed for rapid deployment to austere operating locations. Further, this legacy of Cold War thinking persisted in early EAF concept development in that much initial attention was focused on the deployment of the fighters themselves.

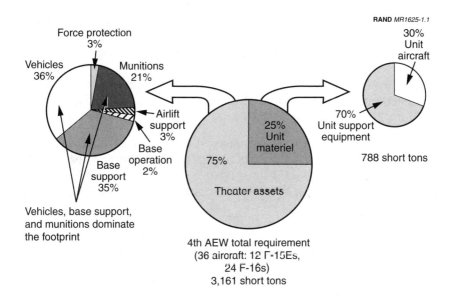

Figure 1.1—Support Footprint for Aerospace Power Is Substantial

---

[5]Theater materiel is provided by organizations outside the combat unit itself. In this case, most was provided by Central Air Forces (CENTAF).

However, a number of studies have examined the support requirements for expeditionary operations. RAND and Air Force researchers have examined the deployability of various support capabilities, including flightline maintenance, avionics repair, Low-Altitude Navigation and Targeting Infrared for Night (LANTIRN) pod maintenance, and jet engine intermediate repair, as well as munitions and fuel support and billeting.[6] The consensus of the research was that moving all the support for an Aerospace Expeditionary Task Force (ASETF)[7] package to the FOL within the notional time frame of 48 hours was almost certainly infeasible given current support process organization and equipment. A 1999 study by Synergy for AF/ILXX also examining movement of a complete support and combat package concluded that it would take about 72 hours to start conducting air-to-ground sorties and as long as 120 hours to reach full operating capability. That study estimated that about 2,500 short tons (including munitions and vehicles, but excluding air defense) would be required to support the 36 ASETF package (an average of 71 short tons per aircraft), and even then the package was heavily tailored from existing support capabilities (at the Unit Type Code (UTC) level). An analysis by Air Force Studies and Analysis (AF/SAA) of movements in Operation Noble Anvil (ONA) suggested that more than 100 short tons per aircraft were required for this operation.[8]

One result of all of this work was a call for "footprint reduction": reducing the amount of materiel and personnel actually deployed to FOLs. According to *AF Vision 2020*: "We will streamline what we take with us, reducing our forward support footprint by 50%." In line

---

[6]See, for example, Vo, 1997; O'Fearna, 1999; Galway et al., 2000; Tripp et al., 2000; Amouzegar et al., 2001; Feinberg et al. 2001a; Peltz et al., 2000; and Killingsworth et al. 2000.

[7]Terminology surrounding the EAF has changed over the five or so years of its existence. Currently, EAF is the overall operational concept, AEFs are the 10 subdivisions of USAF forces, and ASETF is used for whatever force is actually being deployed. However, the acronym AEF was originally used for the deploying force, and it is possible that an entire on-call AEF would be deployed for a major conflict. In this report we use ASETF for the deploying force.

[8]AF/SAA analysts had many caveats for this figure: the substantial infrastructure already available, information missing because of movements outside the Time-Phased Force Deployment Data (TPFDD), and possible contamination of data with the preparation for Operation Poppa Bear, which was a large augmentation of aircraft planned in June 1999 but never executed. Nonetheless, the figure of 100 short tons per aircraft remains a consensus estimate that is consistent with other studies.

with this statement of the problem, much effort and attention has been directed at the physical reduction of support equipment. For example, new and smaller F-15 avionics testers are in development, and new lighter shelters and billeting equipment are being proposed. However, for many areas such as munitions, significant mass reduction will require substantial investment in new technology and development, and for some areas such as civil engineering, large reductions in earth-moving equipment size seem infeasible. As a result, researchers have focused on alternative strategies to physical reduction, such as time-phasing the deployment of support and relocating some processes, equipment, and personnel to locations other than the FOL. The latter work has led to proposals to centralize some of the maintenance and support capabilities for all FOLs in a theater. In some cases, these alternatives are very cost-effective in that they reduce or eliminate the need to purchase new equipment for older combat platforms that are slated for replacement in the next decade or so. Centralization has also helped to reduce the demand on such scarce resources as intertheater airlift and to streamline some of the maintenance processes without reducing the overall capability.[9]

PROJECT OVERVIEW

These efforts at footprint reduction and footprint restructuring led to the formulation of this project in late 2000. The objectives of the study were threefold:

- To define footprint, to establish a baseline whereby progress at reducing footprint could be monitored, and to assess progress to date at restructuring footprint to meet EAF goals;

- To develop an analysis framework for footprint under the EAF concept to assist planners in achieving leaner, more agile deployment by evaluating proposed footprint restructuring (including, but not limited to, physical reduction); and

- To recommend metrics for measuring progress within this framework that relate footprint characteristics to EAF requirements and capabilities.

---

[9]Feinberg et al., 2001b; Amouzegar et al., 2001.

The first objective is taken up in Chapter Two, where progress in footprint reduction is reviewed (with a focus on several key functional areas and their associated deployment packages) and the difficulties in establishing a pre-EAF baseline are discussed. We argue that a sufficiently accurate pre-EAF baseline cannot be established with the available data. Beyond data errors and lack of comparability of pre-EAF combat units with EAF force packages, there is one key shortcoming: There are no comprehensive lists of support requirements for deployed force packages that can provide planners with a list of UTCs needed to initiate operations at a generic base for a given combat scenario.

The analysis framework in the second objective is developed in Chapters Three and Four. Chapter Three, emphasizing the underlying goal of rapid and flexible deployment, introduces a broader concept than footprint, which we call footprint configuration. Footprint configuration extends the conventional notion of footprint—materiel and personnel that must be moved to a base—to one that emphasizes the spatial distribution of the materiel and personnel and the time-phasing of their movement. The chapter ends with a recommendation of metrics for the framework that emphasize the EAF goals.

Chapter Four then outlines some specifications for tools to develop and to evaluate alternative footprint configurations. The final chapter summarizes these findings and offers recommendations for developing and monitoring changes in footprint configuration to achieve EAF deployment goals.

Chapter Two

FOOTPRINT: FROM THE COLD WAR TO THE EAF

As noted in Chapter One, during the Cold War the USAF was primarily poised to respond to conflict in the most volatile arenas of the time: Europe or the Korean peninsula. Since it was likely that the early days in these theaters would be decisive, the USAF established many "warm" bases (fully equipped and often in active use) in these areas. These bases were equipped with prepositioned materiel sufficient to operate without resupply for up to 30 days. Deployment plans largely envisioned the movement of reinforcing aircraft and personnel only, followed by a sustainment phase, if the war continued, during which there would be a substantial movement of replenishment materiel and supplies. This mode of operation was an extension of the largely self-contained bases in the United States from which the Air Force operated in peacetime: Each base contained a complex of maintenance and other support facilities, so that virtually everything needed to support flying was under the direction of the operational commander.

With the advent of the EAF concept, the USAF can no longer assume that most deployments will be to warm bases: The goal of the EAF is to deploy in a short time as needed "anywhere, anytime."[1] This requires that the Air Force be able, if necessary, to deploy fighters to bases with a range of infrastructures, from the warm bases of the Cold War type, to international airports with little military infrastructure, to "bare bases" with no more than water and fuel. In the latter case, the support materiel and personnel required will need to be

---

[1]See U.S. Air Force, 2001, or Sweetman, 2000.

moved to the site and to be operational within 48 hours. Further, in expeditionary operations, advanced support planning must be "generic"—it must apply to a wide range of bases, unlike Cold War planning that developed detailed plans for specific bases.

In the early days of the transition to the EAF structure, attention focused on the movement of the combat aircraft themselves, as vestiges of Cold War thinking still dominated the notion of deployment. But the support materiel and personnel far exceed the mass of the combat aircraft alone. Under current concepts of operation, all the materiel and personnel to initiate and sustain operations—the deployment footprint—must be present for operations to commence, whether prepositioned or moved in. The speed and agility of deployment hinge on the size of this logistical requirement. Hence, with expeditionary operations, a fresh look at footprint is needed to allow faster deployments.

Given that the EAF transformation has been under way for several years, during which time there has been increasing emphasis on reviewing and reducing footprint, it is also important to assess how far the USAF has progressed. We will address that question after a more detailed look at what constitutes footprint.

FOOTPRINT HIERARCHY

The first step in examining footprint and assessing what changes have taken place in the past few years is to recognize that logistics planners work with footprint at three levels. In this report, we will call this the footprint hierarchy and it will serve as an important part of the structure for much of the following discussion. We discuss three levels, illustrated schematically in Figure 2.1:

- The UTC level: a specific support capability (munitions support, jet engine intermediate maintenance (JEIM), avionics repair, etc.), including both materiel and personnel;

- The force/base level: all support capabilities needed to initiate and sustain operations for a given force at an individual base; and

- The theater level: all support capabilities needed over an entire theater given the specific mix of forces and bases.

RAND *MR1625-2.1*

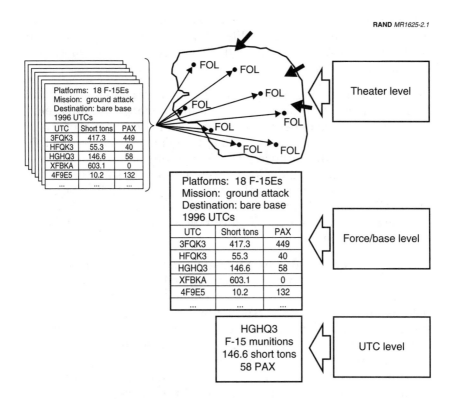

Figure 2.1—Footprint Hierarchy Schematic

UTC Level

The UTC is the basic deployment unit of materiel and personnel in all branches of the U.S. military. Each UTC is a standard, predefined operational or support capability and is designated by a five-character alphanumeric code. The Air Force UTC[2] capabilities are defined in the Mission Capability (MISCAP) statement and their characteristics (people and mass) are listed in the Manpower and Equipment Force Packaging (MEFPAK) system. For example, the UTC 3FQK3 represents an 18 Primary Aircraft Authorized (PAA)

---

[2]In an abuse of language, we will call the package itself a UTC.

F-15E squadron, consisting of 449 people and 417.3 short tons of materiel. It does not include a JEIM shop, so if one is required, an HFQK3 UTC must be deployed with 40 personnel and 55.3 short tons of additional equipment.

In deliberate planning of deployments, each functional area in the Air Force (fuels, munitions, jet engine maintenance, weather, etc.) assembles the capabilities it needs to do its function as a set of UTCs. The MEFPAK descriptions are used in the generation of the TPFDD, which becomes the multiservice deployment list used for transportation planning and deployment execution. In some cases, the entire capability of a standard UTC may not be needed, in which case the UTC is "tailored" by functional area personnel. Such tailored UTCs are often, but not always, given the suffix of "Z99" to indicate that they are not standard.

The development, validation, and maintenance of Air Force UTCs is decentralized to "pilot units"—operating units that do the UTC work as an additional duty.[3] They are responsible for ensuring that the UTC as defined has the personnel and equipment to provide its stated capability. Functional Area Managers (FAMs) at the Major Commands (MAJCOMs) and Air Staff oversee this process, but primarily within functional stovepipes. They focus more on financial control (e.g., advocating allocation of resources for promising modifications in size or functionality). In particular, there is little coordination above the functional area, for example, in looking at the entire set of UTCs that provide a complete base capability (we will return to this point below).[4]

In Operation Desert Storm, many Air Force UTCs arrived with up to 40 percent more personnel and 300 percent more equipment over their nominal values; further, some UTCs did not have their stated capability.[5] This experience, the development of the EAF concept, and further experience in Kosovo spurred a large-scale effort to re-

---

[3]U.S. Air Force, 1999 (Chapter 6), provides details of how UTCs are constructed, entered into service, and maintained, as well as the meaning of the five-character alphanumeric codes.

[4]Hess and Wermund, 1992.

[5]Hagel, 1992.

work all Air Force UTCs.[6] These efforts include "right-sizing" UTCs (redefining standard UTCs to support smaller expeditionary forces in a range of conflicts), instead of relying on custom-tailoring the Cold War era squadron-sized UTCs, which were largely designed for Major Theater Wars (MTWs). A parallel and complementary focus has been to break individual UTCs into modules, so that capabilities can be more precisely fit to specific circumstances.[7] In addition, simultaneous efforts are under way by pilot units and functional area managers to modify UTCs to speed deployment (and hence reduce time to initial operating capability (IOC)), primarily by reducing the weight and personnel in individual UTCs (reducing the footprint). In some areas, attention has moved to broader strategies than these two, which we will describe in more detail below.

Force/Base Level

The second level of the footprint hierarchy, the force/base level, is the total materiel and personnel needed at a base to enable a given deployment of aircraft to achieve a desired combat capability. Notionally, this will be a list of required UTCs determined by the combat force and mission (e.g., an 18-PAA squadron of F-15Es flying air-to-ground bombing missions), the state of the base (e.g., is a civil engineering RED HORSE (Rapid Engineer Deployable Heavy Operations Repair Squadron Engineer) team needed for heavy construction?), and the threat level (e.g., what forces are required to protect the base?).

Overlaid on these scenario dependencies is a temporal dimension: A force/base level list of UTCs can be time-phased (the TPFDD itself is the *time-phased* deployment list). For purposes of footprint analysis, we discuss two timeframes: the time to IOC and the time to full operating capability (FOC). Initiation of combat operations requires that certain materiel and personnel be present (we denote these as the initial operating requirement or IOR), and these UTCs must be

---

[6]U.S. Air Force, n.d.

[7]These efforts were aimed at reducing the number of "tailored" and "Z99" UTCs, leading to easier logistical management and quicker assembly of the TPFDD. This has taken a more significant role, since the ONA TPFDD consisted of 41 percent tailored UTCs and 38 percent Z99 designated UTCs, leaving only 21 percent standard UTCs.

moved first, but other materiel and personnel are only required for sustained operations and can be moved later. We denote the latter materiel and personnel as the full operating requirement or FOR. Judicious time-phasing can decrease time to IOC even though total lift requirements for support are unchanged.

Force/base lists of UTCs are constructed today by deliberate planners at each MAJCOM: For each war plan, functional area managers draw up lists of UTCs based on the force and what is currently prepositioned or otherwise available at each individual beddown base. These plans are tailored to the unique features of the plan and the theater (although they often serve as the starting point for ad hoc or crisis planning).

Theater Level

The third and highest level of footprint hierarchy is the materiel and personnel needed in an entire theater of operations. In the simplest case, this can be the sum of individual force/base footprints. But some support capabilities and supplies can be placed in Forward Support Locations (FSLs).[8] Therefore, analysis at the theater level must take into account economies of scale that alleviate redundancies of capability among bases, create efficiencies in distribution of materiel, and reduce airlift requirements in the crucial initial phase of a deployment.

FOCUS ON FORCE/BASE

Footprint can be reduced at either the theater or UTC level, facilitating improvements in rapid and flexible deployment. UTC-level re-engineering can reduce mass and lead to reduction in airlift for indi-

---

[8]FSL is a generic term that encompasses maintenance, supply, and mobility capabilities located in theater to support multiple FOLs. The implication is that such a facility or set of facilities can be located in more secure areas and can eliminate deployment of some support processes from CONUS to individual FOLs. Such prepositioning is more flexible than prepositioning at selected FOLs themselves. FSLs can also be in continuous operation and hence available at the start of a deployment. These facilities have had several different names in Air Force practice, including Centralized Intermediate Repair Facilities (CIRFs), Regional Support Centers (RSCs), and Regional Supply Squadrons (RSSs).

vidual support processes. Centralized facilities (FSLs) at the theater level can exploit economies of scale and create efficiencies in materiel distribution as reported in RAND's research cited above. But it is a central thesis of this report that the keystone to reducing time to deployment lies in examining the second hierarchical level: the requirements for transforming a base that does not have a full military infrastructure into one that is completely equipped to launch the required combat missions. Furthermore, when computing "progress" made toward reducing footprint, this is the only level that counts: Reductions in individual UTCs are of interest only in reducing the footprint (and hence the deployment time) of a *complete force* deploying to a base. Other strategies such as centralized repair in the theater or from CONUS can also contribute.

Planning and monitoring the progress of footprint reduction at the base level provides a unique vantage point for viewing the levels above (theater) and below (UTC). For example, base-level analysis will expose the illusory gains of reducing the size of one UTC by merely shifting materiel to another; and base-level analysis reveals which UTCs are best targeted for reduction, rather than requiring that each individual FAM achieve equivalent degrees of reduction. Further, understanding the requirements at the base level provides the basic data needed to determine which capabilities and materiel might best be positioned in FSLs in order to exploit economies of scale in a theater composed of many FOLs.

In the following discussion, we will focus on what is needed to bring a bare base to full operational capability. This is the most stressing expeditionary situation: For a given force, a bare base needs the most materiel and personnel to make it operational. The UTCs required would then constitute the most comprehensive list and could then form a baseline in expanding the analysis to include other types of bases. For example, to make a warm base operational, the materiel and processes already in place would be deleted from the bare base list.

To track progress to date in footprint reduction for the EAF, then, the following procedure is suggested:

- Assemble a set of force/base UTC lists for deployment of selected forces to a bare base; and

- Compare the materiel and personnel by using data from the current version of the MEFPAK and one from before the EAF transition that began in 1998.

NEEDED: UTC LISTS FOR FORCE/BASE PACKAGES

Unlike the deliberate planning mentioned above, however, footprint tracking requires *generic* UTC lists that are not tied to specific bases. This is because the whole point of the expeditionary concept is to be ready to deploy to bases that are unprepared. This type of planning has been done to a limited extent. For example, the 366th Wing at Mountain Home AFB is one of the pop-up AEWs charged with being ready to deploy instantly to any warm base worldwide. As part of its planning process, the 366th has developed a list of 120-plus UTCs to augment the support resources at a generic warm base and expects to use the list as a template TPFDD to be completed when deployment begins. Further, since the inception of the EAF, the Air Staff alone has at least twice constructed generic force/base UTC lists specifically to determine footprint size for strategic support planning.[9]

Unfortunately, such comprehensive *generic* UTC lists for bare bases do not seem to exist for any current or proposed force packages outside the pop-up AEWs. The Air Staff efforts were done for exploratory and illustrative purposes, not as an official template for strategic planning. Although clearly *virtual* generic lists exist in the skill base of the functional experts, the lack of a canonical list of support for a given force package leaves logistics planners with few means of orchestrating footprint reduction on a level higher than the UTC.

It might be suggested that the varied deliberate planning TPFDDs and historical data (e.g., from Noble Anvil) could be used in lieu of such generic lists. However, although such efforts provide valuable insight into constructing generic lists, in general these data are not adequate either for tracking progress in footprint reduction or for

---

[9]In early 1999, AF/ILXX contracted with Synergy to estimate the actual time it would take to deploy an entire support package for the canonical AEF (12 F-15Cs, 12 F-15Es, and 12 F-16CGs) to a bare base. Information from extensive interviews with functional area managers was used to list and sequence a set of UTCs. At least one other such exercise was carried out by the Air Staff as preparation for a CORONA briefing.

strategic logistics planning. First, very few of these deployments are to true bare bases, so they do not accurately define the total package required to support any given force. Further, for any historical or planned base and proposed force package, a number of circumstances and assumptions must be taken into account. For example, as we noted above, total deployment figures for bases used in ONA do not shed much information on resources needed to commence operations, and they may be contaminated by the Poppa Bear buildup (in which resources but not aircraft were deployed). Also, the TPFDD for ONA may not include some intratheater movements in Europe that were carried out by civilian transport. In cases drawn from planning data, each base has prepositioned material and assumptions about resources available locally. Figure 2.2 illustrates some of these problems by comparing the total materiel weight in TPFDDs using historical and planning data and the only two generic deployment packages available.

In Figure 2.2, "ONABB" denotes a base used in Noble Anvil that was largely devoid of operating infrastructure except for fuel, water, runways, apron space, and billeting. "InterAirp" is an international airport in CENTAF. "Synerg/ILXX" refers to the UTCs used in the Synergy/ILXX study mentioned above on bare base deployments and "366th" denotes the 366th's planning TPFDD. Synerg/ILXX is the only true bare base in this set. Finally, PACAF is a base used by the Pacific Air Forces (PACAF) that requires a fair amount of deployment to start operations but still has a substantial amount of prepositioned equipment (as do most planned PACAF locations). For each situation, a TPFDD defines the force and the various UTCs deployed. Each cluster of bars shows the proportion of deployment footprint by major category; we used proportion rather than total short tons because the forces deployed to each location are quite different and hence so are the total weights.

Note the wide variation in the packages. No munitions are deployed to the international airport: Presumably, these are either present or will be moved in, but they do not appear in the official TPFDD. The international airport also has a huge amount of bare base support equipment (some of this is prepositioned but still is listed on the TPFDD and hence should be counted as part of the footprint if

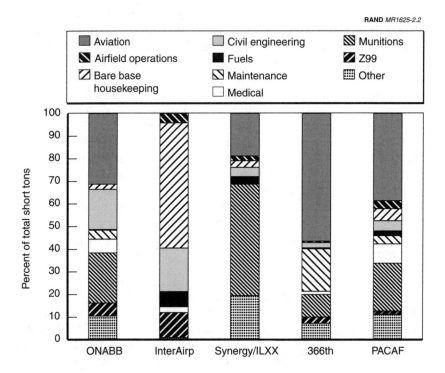

Figure 2.2—Comparison of Selected Planning Footprints

we are trying to define the total package). Also note that civil engineering support is a very small part of the Synergy/ILXX, the 366th, and the PACAF packages but a substantial part of the others. The conclusion must be drawn that without detailed review and editing of deliberate planning or historical TPFDDs, they cannot be used to define the total package required for deploying a combat force.

Finally, many of the UTCs in either deliberate planning or in historical data are heavily modified to delete or add equipment known to be present or absent at the destination or needed or not needed for a particular situation. For example, in the ONA TPFDD used for the AF/SAA analysis, the majority of the UTCs were known to be tailored whereas a number of "standard" UTCs in the TPFDD are also known to have been tailored from a cursory comparison with the description in the MEFPAK. The Synergy/ILXX study also heavily tailored standard UTCs to develop its AEF package.

EXAMPLES OF FUNCTIONAL AREA FOOTPRINT REDUCTION

Because of the lack of a comprehensive UTC list for *any* generic force/base package, we cannot directly estimate the reduction in footprint achieved to date at this level. However, we can illustrate the progress and the resulting current state of UTC reengineering by examining UTC changes in several key functional areas, including four that contribute substantial weight to the total package, especially in deployments to a bare base. Examples are drawn from the following functional areas: bare base support (Harvest Falcon), munitions, civil engineering, and vehicles. We will also examine expeditionary medical UTCs briefly because they illustrate a problem with the UTC approach to reduction and show why the focus should be on the force/base level.

Methodology

We collected data from each functional area to determine what was needed to support deployments of different packages to a bare base[10] and what were the ongoing initiatives to reduce or to modify footprint to help achieve EAF goals. As expected, these packages were largely UTCs.

To compare the characteristics of the UTCs, we used two versions of the MEFPAK. The EAF concept was formally announced in 1998,[11] but we selected the March 1996 MEFPAK for our pre-EAF baseline. According to interviews at AF/ILXX, no MEFPAK was published in 1997 because of data system changes but one was produced in late 1998 and in later years. The consensus was that there were few changes to the Air Force UTCs from Desert Storm until 1998, when

---

[10]In some areas, a deployment package is not strongly linked to the type of mission or even the platforms used. The civil engineering packages are quantified in terms of number of squadrons and the threat level, and the bare base support package is based on the number of people at the FOL.

[11]Ryan, 1998.

the EAF implementation began to accelerate change. For the current UTC characteristics, we used the April 2001 MEFPAK.

Because the 1996 MEFPAK has very few UTCs that pertain to other than squadron-sized forces, the comparisons below are all for forces of this size and above.

Bare Base Support

Aerospace operations from very austere environments require a substantial industrial and billeting infrastructure. This includes power, lighting, water, food, sanitation, and shelter for people and support and operations activities, many of which require computers and other delicate electronic equipment. The current Air Force equipment package to provide such bare base support is called Harvest Falcon[12] and consists of the following three UTCs:

- Housekeeping (XFBKA): This personnel support UTC includes the billeting facilities (primarily tents with environmental control units (ECUs)), power, sanitation, personal hygiene facilities, food preparation, and water treatment.

- Flightline (XFBS1): This UTC provides shelter and utilities such as lighting and power to operations and flightline maintenance.

- Industrial (XFBRB): This UTC provides shelter and utilities for back-shop operations (non-flightline maintenance) and all other base support activities.

This combination is designed to support one fighter squadron (about 1,100 personnel). The XFBKA UTCs have seen hard usage in recent years because they have been used alone both to house personnel at more developed bases, allowing them to be accommodated on base instead of dispersed into local housing, and for refugee shelters in humanitarian operations.

---

[12]Other billeting packages are in use and under development. Among the former, Harvest Eagle packages, which are used in PACAF, are the most common, although these use older technology than Harvest Falcon and are not designed for true bare base operation. Newer packages to support sub-squadron deployments are also under development.

A comparison of Harvest Falcon UTC weights in 1996 and 2001 is shown in Figure 2.3.

There has been a small change in XFBKA, but there has been an enormous change in the other two UTCs, at least when comparing the data in the two different MEFPAKs. We have not been able to find a complete explanation of the change, although the LGX section at the 49th Materiel Management Group (MMG) (the pilot unit for Harvest Falcon UTCs) conjectured that it was due to the addition of B-1 aircraft revetments to protect individual aircraft from attack on the ground. The 49th also confirmed that some of the increase in XFBRB was due to the addition of pipe racks, but even with this addition there were still 400-plus short tons of increase unaccounted for.

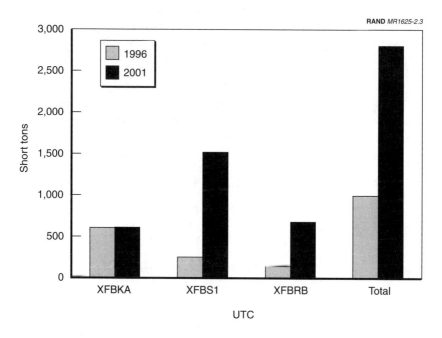

Figure 2.3—Comparison of Harvest Falcon UTCs, 1996 and 2001

The 49th personnel did verify that a recent thorough review of each package showed that the weights in the 2001 MEFPAK are correct.[13]

There is reason to expect some future reductions in the mass of XFBKA, primarily because of the introduction of a new small shelter for billeting and a new ECU, which is 25 percent lighter than just the older tent alone (without ECU) that it replaces. However, the new equipment is more expensive. Similarly, new electricity generation technologies may also make possible further reduction. On the other hand, experience with setting up the package has led to the recommendation that vehicles be considered for inclusion in the package, which would increase its mass.[14]

There has been another innovation in restructuring the mass of the housekeeping UTC, XFBKA, so-called e-Falcon packages. In this concept, the UTC is divided into sub-UTC pieces that can be brought into a bare base in functional segments. Segment A provides basic personnel shelter and some limited facilities such as water purification and power generation, with follow-on segments adding additional facilities. This use of time-phasing allows operations to commence by providing basic shelter for personnel (at a higher billeting density) and then providing additional comfort as the operation proceeds. In addition, the e-Falcon package eliminates some of the heavy packaging (about 45 short tons). Table 2.1 gives the weights of the different segments; the initial

Table 2.1

E-Falcon Component Weights

Package	Weight in Short Tons
A	143.2
B	111.2
C	308.8
Total	563.2

---

[13]Conversation with Capt Paul Smith, logistics plans, at 49th Materiel Management Group, Holloman AFB, New Mexico, July 23, 2001. The 1996 values are close to those in the October 1999 MEFPAK.

[14]Conversation with Col James Lyon, Commander of 49th Materiel Management Group, Holloman AFB, New Mexico, July 20, 2001.

segment is only 24 percent of the original total. This is an example of the division of a capability into IOR (Package A) and FOR (Packages B and C) segments that can be moved into the base at different times.

Munitions

Munitions and related support equipment constitute one of the heaviest areas of materiel. Most of the weight is the munitions, with some additional weight from the equipment and the personnel needed to receive, store, inspect, assemble, and otherwise maintain the munitions. Figure 2.4 compares munitions footprints in 1996 and 2001 for one typical scenario—that of an 18-PAA squadron of F-15Es flying air-to-ground bombing missions. The requirements

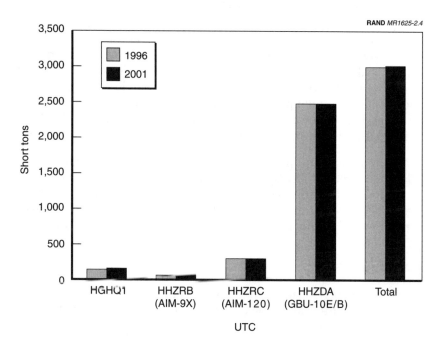

Figure 2.4—Comparison of Munitions UTCs, 1996 and 2001

are calculated for an assumed seven days of operation[15] using GBU-10 laser-guided bombs and AIM-9 (Sidewinder) and AIM-120 (AMRAAM) air-to-air missiles. Munitions weight is based on the nominal weight of the listed weapon plus dunnage. We were unable to use the weights listed in the MEFPAKs for each weapon because of inconsistencies in the munitions UTC codes between the MEFPAKs, or because the needed UTC was under revision and consequently did not list the necessary data in the 2001 MEFPAK. The UTC HGHQ1 provides the needed support in the form of receiving, storage, inspection, maintenance, and handling of the munitions to sustain WMP-5 sortie rates for the F-15E. It includes 66 passengers (PAX) in both the 1996 and 2001 MEFPAKs.

As the figure shows, there has been little change in weight for the total munitions footprint from 1996 to 2001 (there is actually a slight increase in equipment), and the requirements are heavy: roughly 88 short tons per aircraft for the seven-day period for this case. This relatively small change in weight reflects the dominance of bombs and missiles on the total munitions weight and the lack of change in these weapons over the studied period. Indeed, little weight reduction is likely to take place in munitions short of new technologies, such as lighter, more accurate, small diameter bombs (SDBs),[16] which carry their own technological risk in development.

We note that the number of munitions needed for a campaign may also be decreased just by using more precise munitions that reduce the number of bombs that must be dropped to hit a specified target set. Therefore, footprint can also be substantially affected by developments that are not designed to reduce footprint per se.

Civil Engineering

Civil engineers (CE) are trained military engineers who provide initial beddown facilities assembly, fire protection, disaster preparedness,

---

[15]Munitions requirements were calculated using RAND's spreadsheet munitions model. See Tripp et al., 1999; Amouzegar et al., 2000.

[16]This 250-lb munition is expected to successfully attack 70 percent of the targets that currently require a 2,000-lb bomb, but, as of this writing, it is not expected to be available until 2007.

explosive ordnance disposal (EOD), base recovery, and sustainment support for flying operations. In a deployment to a bare base, CE Prime BEEF (Prime Base Engineer Emergency Force) teams set up temporary housing, kitchen, sanitation, water distribution, power generation, and runway lighting. They also maintain these facilities, provide fire protection for flight operations, and provide for EOD and full spectrum nuclear, biological, and chemical (NBC) threat protection.

The UTCs for civil engineer, as with other functional areas, have undergone reengineering to be more responsive to the requirements of the EAF. This has primarily involved the division of Prime BEEF teams into smaller UTC packages to permit phased deployment and to allow fewer engineers to be deployed for less than squadron-sized deployments and for cases in which deployments are to warm bases with existing engineers and support equipment. The structure of these UTCs is somewhat complex and will not be described in detail here.[17] Figures 2.5 and 2.6 compare (by CE area) the equivalent squadron support package for a low-threat condition in 1996 and 2001. Additional squadrons primarily require more engineers, whereas higher-threat conditions require more EOD and readiness technicians.

From Figures 2.5 and 2.6, we can see some minor increases in equipment mass for several categories and some minor decreases in personnel. The major change is a substantial increase in the number of firefighters and amount of firefighting equipment. This increase has resulted from a decision to provide firefighting protection in a deployment equal to U.S. standards for firefighting at airfields. This requires enough equipment and personnel to protect the largest aircraft commonly at the base with a sufficient volume of fire-retarding foam to suppress and to put out a fire involving this type of aircraft. Each type of aircraft requires a fixed number of trucks and this in turn translates directly into the number of crews required for 24-hour manning. In the case of fighter bases, the requirement that drives the 2001 UTCs is that the base be able to handle fires on the C-130; in 1996, the requirement was only to be able to handle fires on fighter aircraft.

---

[17]U.S. Air Force, 2000.

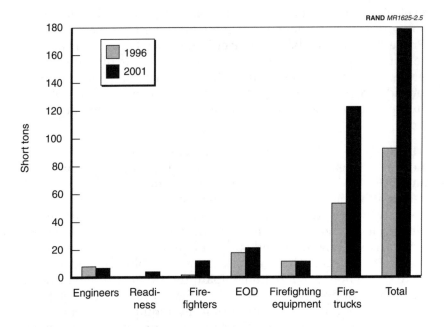

RAND *MR1625-2.5*

**Figure 2.5—Comparison of Short Tons Required for CE Bare Base
Deployment, 1996 and 2001**

This illustrates the problems of trading off risk and footprint reduction: The new concepts of centralizing some maintenance and other functions and linking FOLs together with intratheater transport aircraft (primarily C-130s) would seem to validate the need for increased fire protection at the FOLs. On the other hand, even this increased firefighting capability would not be able to handle fires on intertheater aircraft such as the C-5 or C-17 during the early phases of a deployment.

In more general terms, the danger in reengineering a functional area such as civil engineering for smaller footprint is that this functional area is an enabler. It sets up the base to allow operations to proceed. Fewer engineers may reduce the engineering footprint but increase the time to IOC and FOC for the full squadron. It is conceivable that it might sometimes be advisable to *increase* the CE footprint to reduce time to IOC or FOC.

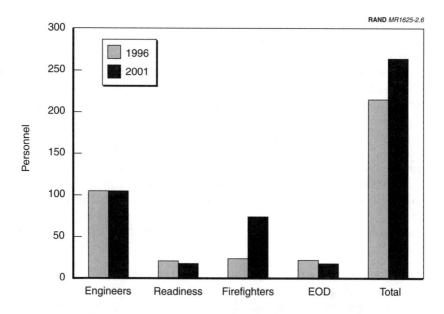

Figure 2.6—Comparison of Personnel Required for CE Bare Base
Deployment, 1996 and 2001

If a base requires more than just bare base construction (such as major runway repair or building, or significant construction), the UTCs to do this are RED HORSE teams. Each component of these teams (heavy construction, runway repair, etc.) has 120 to 150 people and hundreds of tons of heavy construction equipment. Unfortunately, the heavy equipment needed for these teams will remain heavy and cannot be reduced without reducing the capability of the team. The civil engineers plan either to centralize the use and deployment of RED HORSE teams for a theater deployment or to arrange for contractors or other entities in specific regions or for specific bases to provide the heavy equipment. This can dramatically reduce the footprint moved to an FOL but it will increase the risk of losing access to equipment because of threats or political restrictions.

Vehicles

Numerous vehicles are required to set up the housing, sanitation, food service, aircraft revetments, etc., in a bare base deployment. These are not considered part of the civil engineering Prime BEEF UTCs although, as noted above, some vehicles are being considered for inclusion in the Harvest Falcon packages. It is somewhat surprising to note that there is no standard list of vehicles for a bare base deployment. This is due partly to the Air Force's focus on deliberate planning for specific operations noted above: Most bases to which the Air Force plans to deploy have some vehicles available so that each deployment requires a different list of vehicles tailored to the specific base. Many of these are general-purpose vehicles that can be provided through local contracting, and since many are trucks and forklifts of various sizes, they are shared among different functions.

As we have argued above, a standard list of needed vehicles is useful because strategic logistics planning requires knowing what to include in a generic bare base deployment. To date, the best candidate that we can find for such a catalog is a list of 61 vehicles in the current *Guide to Bare Base Development*.[18] (The list is identified as UTC UFSWA, but this was apparently never recorded as a formal UTC.) The total size of the package for one squadron is 522.8 short tons (excluding fire trucks and water carriers that we have included in the CE materiel above). Additional squadrons would require more transportation vehicles, up to a total of 653.1 short tons for three squadrons.

Medical

The medical functional area has been one of the most aggressive in reducing and restructuring its footprint. However, one of its efforts illustrates some of the problems that a purely functional area approach to footprint reduction can raise and reinforces the need to evaluate any footprint changes in terms of the total support for a combat unit.

---

[18] U.S. Air Force, 1996, Annex D.

The pre-EAF medical support system consisted of air transportable hospitals (ATHs). For a squadron, the required facility was a 25-bed ATH that requires three C-17s to move (roughly 135 short tons). Basically, the complete ATH was the IOR *and* FOR for medical care. As a result of new equipment and rethinking of how much support needs to be in place at what time, the Air Force medical community devised a series of packages, starting with a two-person advance team (a physician and a public health officer), to a small, self-deployable surgical team, to an expeditionary medical support (EMEDS) facility that can be built up in segments and requires only 54 short tons (1.3 C-17s).

However, the EMEDS's mass was reduced by removing generators from it, abandoning its traditional power self-sufficiency and requiring it to draw its power from the bare base power grid. This, however, runs counter to the e-Falcon initiative of reducing generating capability to reduce the Falcon package weight. As the authors of the *Bare Base Annual Report 2000*[19] put it, getting rid of the EMEDS power generation does not reduce footprint if someone else has to absorb the load. The effect of any action must be gauged by the effect on the entire base package, not just within the functional area.[20]

MEASURING FOOTPRINT REDUCTION

Figure 2.7 shows the sum of the masses of the four major areas discussed above.

It is clear that there has been a slight increase in footprint in munitions and CE, but the biggest change by far is that found in the bare base support sets. The total for these four areas increased 53 percent between 1996 and 2001. As we noted above, there is some ambiguity in how much of this is due to data errors and how much to the actual addition of equipment, although some of the latter is certainly responsible. Note that for an 18-PAA squadron, the increase works out to 283 short tons per aircraft, even though the expendable

---

[19]*Bare Base Annual Report 2000*, ACC/LGXW, December 1, 2000, Rev A, December 26, 2000.

[20]As of this writing (mid-2002), a generator sufficient for initial operation has been restored to the EMEDS package.

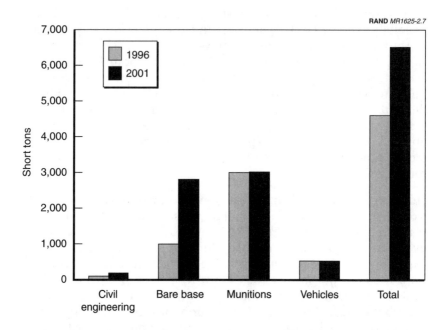

Figure 2.7—Comparison of Four Major Footprint Components, 1996 and 2001

munitions are for only a seven-day operation. In addition, even if the number of aircraft supported is doubled, the number of short tons per aircraft is still substantially more than 100. This does not include another bare base housekeeping set (which would probably be needed) or more munitions (although this addition would probably not be significant, since the munitions computed above for F-15E ground attack would constitute most of the weight, even if other aircraft were added).

The lack of a comprehensive UTC list for bare base deployments restricts our ability to quantify total footprint, but footprint in our illustrations together totals over 5,000 short tons, which would be a substantial amount of the deployment footprint for a squadron. From the discussion above, we conclude that footprint has probably slightly *increased* from 1996. This is shown in Figure 2.8, which compares the UTCs from the 1996 and 2001 MEFPAKs that are (1) in both MEFPAKs, (2) have the same code, and (3) have the same

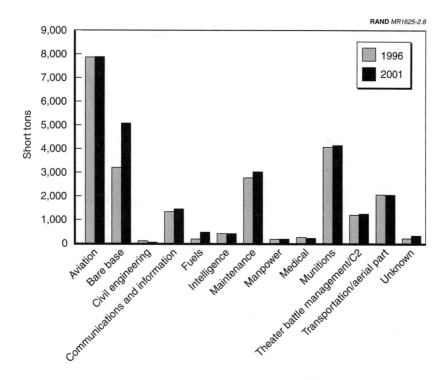

Figure 2.8—Comparison of UTCs, 1996 and 2001

description. In this figure, each bar represents the total mass of those UTCs in the broad category that meets the specified criteria.

The only area to show a decrease is civil engineering (although we know from the analysis above that some specific UTCs of interest to us from Prime BEEF did in fact increase).

We therefore argue that an attempt to establish a "pre-EAF" baseline is not worthwhile. First, in the absence of a UTC list that has been validated and tested and can generate force packages by specifying parameters such as aircraft and missions, it is difficult to establish a credible complete footprint. Second, even with such a list, UTC data, especially in older MEFPAKs, are of doubtful quality (e.g., the Harvest Falcon UTCs) and the chances of correcting data errors are small because of personnel turnover and lack of record-keeping as to contents, changes, corrections, etc. Third, recent deployment TPFDDs have included aggressively tailored of UTCs without retaining information about how much is available at the bases, thus rendering the TFPDD problematic as a source of baseline information. Finally, it will be difficult to acquire other MEFPAKs because historical versions are incompletely archived.[21]

We argue that the best course of action for the Air Force is to

- Focus on developing UTC lists parameterized by mission variables that can be used for strategic expeditionary support planning. This is a key core competency for expeditionary operations.

- Use this capability to begin tracking progress toward meeting the expeditionary deployment goal from today's force.

In the next chapter, we discuss in more detail what is required in a parameterized UTC list and expand the concept of footprint to explore alternative and complementary strategies for speeding deployment rather than simply physically reducing footprint.

---

[21]Conversation with MSgt Larry Leach, AF/ILXX, July 23, 2001.

Chapter Three

BEYOND FOOTPRINT: FOOTPRINT CONFIGURATION

BACK TO THE GOAL: TIME TO COMBAT CAPABILITY

In Chapter One, we emphasized that the primary goal in developing expeditionary support concepts is to speed the deployment of aerospace capability so that it can be employed quickly and sustained as necessary. There is certainly scope for footprint reduction as defined in the previous chapter and physical reduction is an important tool in achieving the deployment goal, but the analyses in Chapter Two suggest that in some cases there is probably limited scope for near-term reductions in actual mass. For example, bulldozers are heavy pieces of equipment because of their function and probably cannot be substantially reduced in size. This is recognized and many of the efforts under way to reduce footprint actually involve not the physical reduction of weight but rather restructuring footprint, time- and space-phasing appropriate parts of it, and analyzing the risks involved in certain reduction strategies.

To include these other strategies in making decisions about restructuring support to enhance deployment, we need a broader concept for the size of support. Such a new concept will help in analyzing the time and resources needed to deploy support processes, particularly at the force/base level. We develop such a framework below, which we call footprint configuration. However, an essential precondition to doing this analysis at the force/base level is development of a comprehensive capability-based list of support processes and the materiel and personnel they require. As we discussed in Chapter Two, such a list does not now exist for use as a planning tool. Because this tool is essential in analyzing footprint configurations for expeditionary operations, we discuss it first before describing the concept of footprint configuration itself.

PARAMETERIZED UTC LISTS

If the USAF is to become truly expeditionary—able to move to locations of varying degrees of austerity and to set up operations quickly—it must be able to enumerate accurately the resources it needs to move and the time needed to become operational. Operators and planners should be able to assess, in advance, the requirements to bed down a specific force in various kinds of locations. In the expeditionary mode, moreover, there will often be little time for deliberate planning, preliminary visits, or extensive transportation feasibility studies. "Saving valuable airlift" by extensive tailoring of UTCs will have to be traded off against quick response.

To achieve this, the Air Force will have to develop the capability to assemble lists of UTCs for different force packages to deploy to generic locations. Such lists will serve as a starting point for tailoring for deliberate planning and a basis for strategic support and deployment planning. Such parameterized lists will also be required for the top-down perspective on footprint reengineering at the force/base that we will present below, in that it will allow decisionmakers to examine *all* components of a deployment package to allocate resources for restructuring and reduction.

As noted in the previous chapter, this need has surfaced before; several times, the Air Staff has been asked to estimate the footprint for moving an ASETF to a bare base.[1] MAJCOM planning staffs have expressed concern about wide variation in estimates given for such a movement, even for similar units replacing each other in rotations. In most cases, these variations have been resolved with ad hoc analyses of historical deployments or war plans.

We suggest that the ad hoc assemblages be replaced with a systematic set of parameterized UTC lists that would specify deployment packages for sets of forces and missions. The determining parame-

---

[1]Conversation with Lt Col Frank Gorman, AF/ILXX, June 11, 2001.

ters would also include components of destination infrastructure and threat level, among others. Such capability-based lists could be used for strategic planning of transportation resources, a starting point for footprint changes (identifying large UTCs that are natural candidates for reduction or restructuring, accounting for materiel shifted out of one UTC to another without acknowledging that no total reduction has been achieved), and a template against which deliberate and crisis planning for specific locations could be compared. As noted above, the 366th Composite Wing at Mountain Home has done exactly this; its list is designed to be generic for deployment to a warm base.

FOOTPRINT CONFIGURATION

The next task, after developing parameterized UTC lists for generic or specific planning scenarios—using information on forces, base infrastructure, mission, threat conditions, etc.—is to develop a methodology to help reduce the deployment timeline for a specific combat capability. We argued above that simple weight reduction, although feasible in some areas, is only one strategy among many and may not be appropriate or easily achievable in areas such as munitions or civil engineering. This insight is borne out both by the RAND research cited above on centralization of some repair activities and by the restructuring of capability based on the time-phasing of support deployment proposed in areas such as medical and bare base support. In this section, we present a broader view of footprint that we have called *footprint configuration.* It provides a framework for visualizing and assessing this broader array of strategies.

The term "footprint" is often restricted in general Air Force usage to materiel that is moved to an FOL to commence operations. However, in many places substantial prepositioned materiel is already in storage at many FOLs. This is seldom considered as footprint and yet it enhances deployment time by reducing the materiel that needs to be moved to reach a desired capability. Similarly, strategies such as centralization of some repair facilities, or moving support capability to FOLs only as needed, can also speed deployment, even when total deployed materiel is not reduced at all but just allocated between the FOL and the centralized facilities. We follow this line of reasoning to develop the concept of footprint configuration.

Forward Operating Location versus Remote Support Processes

Previous researchers have observed that support processes[2] (or pieces of such processes) can be divided into those that must be done at an FOL from which aircraft fly and those that can be done remotely, either at FSLs or even at CONUS Support Locations (CSLs).[3] For example, avionics Line Replaceable Unit (LRU) removal and replacement must be done on the aircraft, and so flightline avionics maintenance personnel and their equipment must be located at the FOL. In contrast, LRU repair can be done off base, provided that there are adequate spares to cover the repair pipeline when it is extended by transportation. As noted by Peltz and Feinberg and their collaborators,[4] this can result in substantial reductions in the initial transportation capacity required and was used to good effect in Operation Noble Anvil.[5]

The equipment (or personnel) footprint can therefore be initially divided into two pieces as illustrated in Figure 3.1.

RAND *MR1625-3.1*

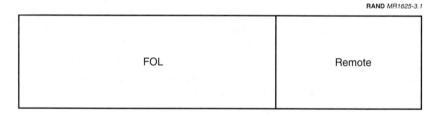

Figure 3.1—Division of Footprint into FOL and Remote Pieces

---

[2]In this project, we focused on support processes because their mass dominates the traditional footprint, but much of the subsequent discussion holds true for the operational part of footprint as well. Restructuring these capabilities along the lines discussed here has been examined in some of the literature on expeditionary operations.

[3]Peltz et al., 2000; Galway et al., 2000. Note that a substantial portion of F-16 avionics is supported by a two-level concept (depot and flightline).

[4]Peltz et al., 2000.

[5]Feinberg et al., 2001a.

The FOL Segment

The FOL segment can in turn be subdivided into three pieces as shown in Figure 3.2:

The three subdivisions are as follows:

- The IOR is required at the FOL to initiate combat operations (bring the base to IOC).

- The FOR is needed at the FOL to sustain combat operations at the desired tempo (bring the base to and maintain it at FOC).

- The on-call segment is required at an FOL only in specific (and implicitly rare) circumstances.

To make these ideas concrete, we will use munitions support as an illustration. The initial operating requirement for munitions consists of an initial stockpile of munitions, fins and fuzes plus the munitions assembly, and movement equipment. The follow-on requirement would be the resupply of munitions necessary to continue carrying out operations. The on-call category could include specialized fuzes or nose guards that may be used for a very specific mission. These are light and small enough (and perhaps expensive enough) to be airlifted to the FOL only as needed.

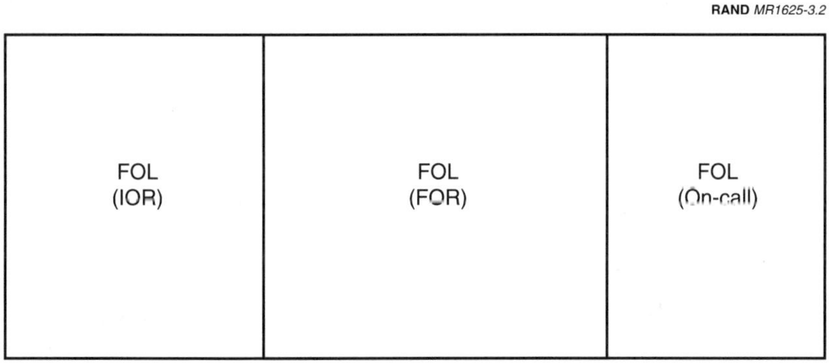

RAND *MR1625-3.2*

| FOL (IOR) | FOL (FOR) | FOL (On-call) |

Figure 3.2— Subdivision of FOL Footprint Portion into IOR, FOR, and On-Call

The on-call category can be further illustrated by using the "cobra crane" as an example. This heavy piece of equipment is needed for repairing canopies. If such a repair is expected to be rare, the crane could be brought in only if needed, at the risk of not being able to do a canopy repair quickly. Similarly, some of civil engineering's heavy repair capability, such as the teams and equipment for runway repair, may be brought in only *after* a runway has been damaged. This might be a worthwhile risk if the enemy had limited ability to attack a runway, or if the capability could be moved quickly to an FOL with ground transportation.

The Remote Segment

The remote segment, in turn, can be subdivided into two pieces as in Figure 3.3.

- FSLs can support FOLs with selected maintenance or supply processes and are linked to the FOLs, by intratheater transport (C-130 or similar aircraft, or, where applicable, ground or sea transport).

- CSLs are support facilities in the CONUS that are linked to FOLs by intertheater transportation (C-5s, C-17s, and long-range commercial cargo aircraft).

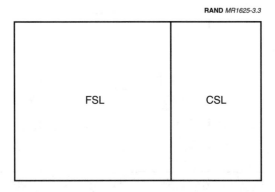

RAND *MR1625-3.3*

Figure 3.3—Subdivision of Remote Footprint Portion into
Portions at Forward and CONUS Support Locations

Examples of FSLs would be the CIRFs established during Operation Noble Anvil at locations such as RAF Lakenheath and Spangdahlem in Germany to support FOLs in Italy and Turkey with avionics and engine repair and phase maintenance. Currently, many F-16 avionics LRUs are repaired by CONUS facilities no matter where the aircraft are located around the world.

Putting It All Together: Footprint Configuration

An amalgamation of these subdivisions gives a time- and space-phasing of the different segments of this notional process as it is required to support operations at the FOL. The shading in each segment of Figure 3.4 shows what is prepositioned, giving a comprehensive picture of what needs to be moved and when. The subdivisions imply spatial distribution, sequencing and priority, and time of delivery.

We have presented the discussion so far in terms of a single support process. However, the real interest is in combining all support processes into a force/base package, as shown in Figure 3.5.

We expect that different support processes have different subdivisions. Some may need to be entirely at the FOL, with no part that can even be on-call (e.g., notional support process B). Others may not have any part at a CSL (process E); in others, the proportion in each segment may vary, along with what can be prepositioned (the shaded areas). In contrast, the traditional view of footprint merely

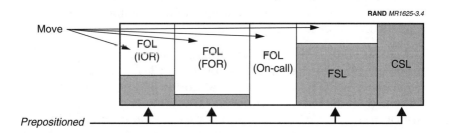

Figure 3.4—Footprint Configuration for a Notional Individual Support Process

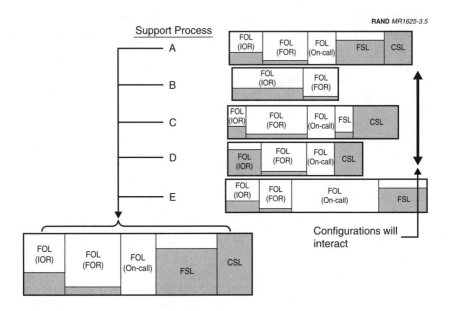

Figure 3.5—Combining Footprint Configurations for Multiple Support Processes

considers materiel initially deployed to an FOL (i.e., the unshaded portion of the FOL (IOR) segment). Failure to consider the many dimensions of footprint may lead to incorrect estimation of requirements for some support processes as well as inefficient utilization of scarce lift capability. The concept of footprint configuration allows for the traditional reduction in weight and personnel while encompassing the other strategies as well.

Footprint configuration allows different process configurations to interact, either at the force/base or theater level. If an FSL can be established with robust transportation for jet engine intermediate repair, then an FSL for avionics at the same location can use the transportation links that have already been established. So, in making decisions about how to reconfigure a process, all levels of the footprint hierarchy need to be considered.

METRICS FOR EVALUATING FOOTPRINT CONFIGURATIONS

One advantage of the traditional concept of footprint was that its measurement was conceptually simple: mass of materiel and number of people to be moved.[6] In contrast, because the basis of footprint configuration is to structure support processes across space and time, the characteristics of footprint configuration are multidimensional. The primary goal to be satisfied is speed of deployment for IOR and FOR so that a given needed capability can reach IOC and FOC, but transportation resources, risk, and a variety of costs need to be weighed as well. We defer any consideration of *how* these tradeoffs are to be made until Chapter Four; here we enumerate and discuss *which* metrics need to be considered.

There are four primary metrics:

- **Time to IOC** and **time to FOC** for the desired capability. These are the key goal for expeditionary operations: The force must be deployed and be operational within the time required to deal with a developing crisis and it must be sustainable to be credible.

- **Transportation resources required to move the IOR** and **transportation resources required to move the FOR.** Unless these are "feasible" (in the sense of being acceptable to the theater combatant commanders) under a variety of circumstances, expeditionary aerospace forces will not be used. For crises, the first is probably more important, whereas in major regional conflicts, the second would be as or more important.

Achieving desired values on these four metrics require trading off and controlling several other key metrics:

- **Materiel mass and personnel moved.** As with footprint alone, these are still important aspects of support processes beyond their direct effect on deployment time, because materiel and

---

[6]As we noted in Chapter Two, this perception is simplistic. Widespread use of prepositioning meant that risks and costs for maintenance and storage were involved, although they were rarely made explicit.

personnel at FOLs are exposed to greater (or at least different forms of) threat.

- **Cost.** Both investment and recurring costs are important. Investment costs are expenses incurred to set up a capability, such as purchase of materiel, land, and construction costs. Recurring costs include the costs of security, maintenance, and periodic exercises.

- **Flexibility.** Is the configuration chosen able to support different kinds of operations under varying circumstances? Too much prepositioning could reduce the flexibility to use other FOLs.

- **Risk.** A series of risk analyses need to be done for any configuration, including risks of depending on transportation, the vulnerability of FOLs with prepositioned materiel and of centralized facilities, political risk, cost risk, and technical risks.

- Finally there is the **effect on the current peacetime** force of pursuing a given set of reconfigurations.

For many of these metrics, input from the operations side of the Air Force will be required. How much flexibility is needed and how much can be traded for speed and robustness? What risks are acceptable and unacceptable? What is IOC/IOR? What are the missions and operational rates needed? The close linkage between operations and logistics that is forged by expeditionary operations presents a new challenge for the Air Force.[7]

It is a given in complex decisionmaking that when a number of different metrics and goals are to be simultaneously satisfied, tradeoffs and compromises will be inevitable. As noted in Galway et al., 2000, and Tripp et al., 2000, to accomplish fast deployments with today's support processes would require extensive prepositioning that is both expensive and carries significant political and military risks. Stocking FSLs with War Reserve Materiel (WRM) in theater can reduce some of the risks and costs, but at the price of longer deployment times and the dependence on assured transportation.

---

[7]Tripp et al., 2000.

To make these tradeoffs rigorously requires several different capabilities. First, all aspects of support must be accounted for. This is the role of parameterized UTC lists discussed above. Second, for any proposed configuration, we need the capability to evaluate the above metrics (and any additional ones deemed necessary). Third, we need to be able to rank and weight the metrics so that we can make tradeoffs based on their value to decisionmakers (some high costs may be paid to get a substantial decrease in deployment time).

Although this project did not attempt to build actual decision support tools to implement these capabilities, in the next chapter we discuss some ideas about making these evaluations and tracking progress. In that chapter, we point out that this process of reconfiguring footprint and making tradeoffs requires both bottom-up and top-down perspectives: bottom-up for technical expertise in a given process and top-down to ensure that any tradeoffs made enhance overall performance and do not suboptimize one area at a cost to the whole.

Chapter Four

DEVELOPING, EVALUATING, AND TRACKING
ALTERNATIVE FOOTPRINT CONFIGURATIONS

As noted above, the goal of rethinking footprint is to speed deployment and to reduce the use of transportation resources. Physical footprint reduction is only one of several strategies to help achieve this goal, but evaluating complementary strategies such as time-phasing, support from FSLs, and other methods that extend processes beyond the FOLs requires a strategic and often cross-functional perspective that can focus on high-payoff areas, assess technical risks, allocate resources, and track performance. Footprint configuration, the concept introduced in Chapter Three, provides a framework for developing and evaluating such strategies.

TOOLS FOR RECONFIGURING FOOTPRINT

To implement the reconfiguration of footprint, two related types of tools are required:

- *Evaluation tools* to help make strategic support decisions. Given a proposed footprint configuration and a set of forces and base infrastructures, these tools evaluate the configuration in terms of the relevant metrics such as time to deployment, weight, investment costs, and risk. This allows decisionmakers to rank alternative configurations and to select those that perform well.

- *Tracking tools* to follow the progress in attaining expeditionary deployment goals for specific force/base combinations, key UTCs, and key theater warplans to assess how close the Air Force is to achieving its expeditionary goals.

As we argued in Chapter Two, the primary focus should be on evaluating and tracking key force/base combinations (the middle level of the footprint hierarchy), since these are the fundamental building blocks of expeditionary deployments. Although theater characteristics play a major role in determining force/base configurations (e.g., the presence or absence of FSLs is obviously an important determinant of what needs to be moved to the FOLs), once these decisions are made, theater evaluation and tracking are essentially an aggregation of the force/base evaluation and tracking. Similarly, although UTC evaluation and tracking are fundamental to implementation of footprint configuration, their role is diagnostic in helping to focus resources and attention on limiting factors affecting performance at the force/base level.

In the rest of this chapter we will lay out the set of tools required for each level of the hierarchy. In the course of this project, we have developed some prototype tools for specific parts of the problem—tools that indicate what can be done to provide more comprehensive analysis. Where we have not done actual prototyping (especially in the area of tracking), we provide some ideas about the form of the tools required and give some suggestions about what should be tracked.

EVALUATING AND TRACKING FORCE/BASE PACKAGES

As we have argued above, the key requirement for evaluating force/base packages is the ability to assemble the list of UTCs that need to be deployed to the base to support the force to be bedded down. The list needs to be parameterized by both force characteristics (platform, mission, sortie rates) and by available FOL infrastructure (shelter, fuel supply system, etc.). For individual functional areas, a few other conditions need to be factored into the generation of the deployment list (e.g., threat level for force protection and civil engineering).

We developed a prototype of this type of model for civil engineering. The model begins with data describing the complete list of civil engineering UTCs. Data for each UTC item include a description of the capability, its weight in short tons, associated personnel, bulk weight, and outsize and oversize requirements for lift. To this, we added data to further categorize the civil engineering UTC items in terms of organization and function, e.g., Prime BEEF teams, RED HORSE teams, and RED HORSE equipment, firefighting teams and equipment, EOD teams and equipment, and readiness teams and equipment. Scenario inputs of the model define the assumptions about FOL capabilities, prepositioned equipment, and threat level. Rules built into the model define the conditions under which particular civil engineering UTCs are selected and the quantity of these to be included in the deployment package. For example, the rules would define the specific Prime BEEF UTCs and quantities for one deployed squadron to an FOL requiring the setup of bare base facilities. The number of readiness team UTCs would depend on the selected specified level of threat. If heavy construction were required in the scenario, the appropriate RED HORSE team UTCs would be added. If the scenario called for follow-on squadrons, requiring increments of Prime BEEF support, the appropriate follow-on UTC would be added to the deployment list. Figure 4.1 illustrates the process in the abstract; actual use of the spreadsheet to evaluate the deployment performance of different packages requires selection of a scenario and other parameters. The development and use of this type of automated deployment list process is crucial to the evaluation of improvements in footprint configuration and should be useful for quickly developing at least preliminary TPFDD lists for real deployments.

Evaluation

Given a similar capability for all support (and operational) areas, a list of UTCs could be generated for any given force/base package. Building on these data, an evaluation tool could allow decisionmakers to modify the deployment list by selecting new or alternative UTCs or by modifying selected UTCs (based on UTC-specific reengineering) to allow pieces of UTCs to be time-phased, prepositioned, or deployed to an FSL instead of the FOL. Such decisions would change the ultimate package deployed and would be reflected in the key metrics of time to IOC and deployment resources computed by the tool. Figure 4.2 shows the notional structure of the broader tool. A set of requirements models for different support processes sit at the center (and interact, so that personnel changes in one support area, for example, are reflected in billeting). Requirements parameters (force and mission characteristics, technological changes, etc.)

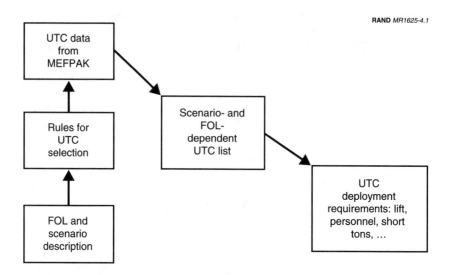

RAND *MR1625-4.1*

Figure 4.1—Model Process to Develop UTC Lists for Specific Scenarios and FOL Characteristics

are inputs to the model, and the outputs are, depending on the support options chosen, the size and movement requirements. This type of model could be used to examine the effect of process changes, support options, and technological innovations.[1]

In some sense, this is like a TPFDD generation system (and could be built from one), although the aim here is to look at overall measures of deployment and make decisions among alternative strategies to improve those measures.

After evaluation, one configuration (choice of FSL functions, prepositioning, technological development) must be selected. To select one that performs well across the multiple metrics proposed, the RAND-developed DynaRank Decision Support System[2] is ideal. This tool, an EXCEL add-on, is a scorecard development tool; it allows the

---

[1]Tripp et al., 1999.

[2]Hillestad and Davis, 1998.

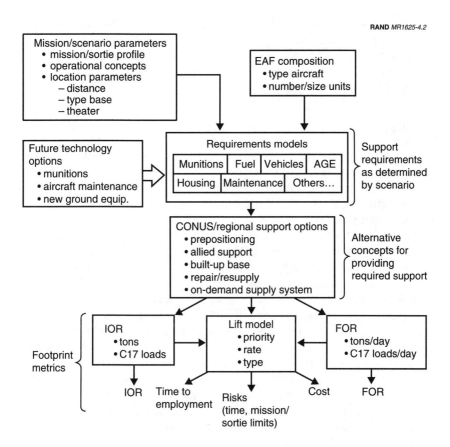

RAND *MR1625-4.2*

Figure 4.2—Evaluation Tool for Force/Base Package

user to specify a hierarchy of metrics (which appear as columns), and options to be compared (which appear as rows). This forms the basis for the desired scorecard structure. The cells corresponding to performance of the given option on a single metric can then be filled in automatically by tying models of the type described earlier or other databases to the DynaRank scorecard. Scorecard manipulation functions allow the decisionmaker, who has control over which metrics are most important, to select multiple options to be sorted, ranked, and displayed by individual metric performance or aggregate weighted performance. Cost can be treated as a special metric if cost-effectiveness comparisons are desired. With DynaRank, different footprint configurations can be evaluated and decisionmakers can select those that provide the best expeditionary support.

Tracking

Once specific footprint configuration decisions have been made, tracking progress at the force/base level is then straightforward. As footprint configuration changes are implemented (new technology, new equipment, the development of FSLs with a corresponding reduction in support process components that are positioned at the FOL), the amount of materiel that needs to be deployed for IOR will decrease and so will time to IOC and deployment resources required. It is useful to organize the configuration options and improvements into a scorecard type of display that shows how they "score" on many of the metrics. The scorecard can also be used to show performance on measures that are more subjective, such as risk and flexibility. Additional rows to the illustrated scorecard would show and track additional years as further improvements or changes are made in footprint configuration. Of course, it will be important to keep operations, FOL capabilities, and threat conditions the same in the multiyear comparisons because changes in assumptions about these may have a much larger effect on footprint configuration performance than improvements in the configuration.

Such changes can be represented to senior decisionmakers either in graphical or tabular form (Table 4.1).

The final question is which force/base packages need to be tracked. For the near future, the warm base type of infrastructure will continue to be important, especially for forces such as the 366th AEW. For fast-breaking operations to areas where warm bases are not prepared, the international airport base infrastructure will be key. The stated goal of the EAF, of course, is to be able to deploy even to very austere bare bases, but the analysis presented in previous chapters and the other research cited indicate that the timelines to deploy a

Table 4.1

Tabular Tracking of Force/Base Package (Notional)

			Footprint			Time (hrs)		Resources
Year	Force	Base	Short Tons	PAX	Short Tons/ Aircraft	IOC	FOC	Transport-ation (C-17 Equiv.)
2001	F-15E ground attack w/ GBU-10	Bare	5089.4+	1100	283+	105+		113
2003	F-15E ground attack w/ GBU-10	Bare	4569.3+	950	253.8+	90+		101

substantial force to such a base is currently somewhat outside the notional goal.[3]

For fighter packages, current planning suggests that the following are the most important:

- Full squadrons of F-15Es (ground attack), F-16CJs for suppression of enemy air defenses (SEAD) and either or both F-15s and F-16s for air-to-air.

- The "canonical" ASETF: 12 each of F-15Es, F-15Cs, and F-16CJs, for a small, balanced package of capability.

- A six-ship package of F-15s or F-16s for air-to-air.[4]

It would also be of interest to consider airlift, surveillance/ reconnaissance, and bomber deployments (the 366th has done the latter in its deployment planning). The combination of the three base infrastructures with the force/mission packages above should

---

[3]This is true for fighter-intensive packages. Of course, the types of force packages that are deployed to bare bases could be kept small or restricted to humanitarian-type operations, with a corresponding reduction in time to IOC.

[4]This stems from the parallel interest of the Air Force in dispersed operations; current thinking appears to be that forces should be dispersed in such a way as to provide four-ship flights from a single location, which means a six-ship deployment. This is *not* official Air Force policy at this time and is the subject of much discussion.

provide a comprehensive view of how well the Air Force could carry out expeditionary operations over a wide spectrum of situations.

One final point of emphasis: This tracking should be done in terms of *generic* deployments, not actual ones. In this way, attention is focused on the strategic problems of expeditionary support, not on details of specific bases and units. We expect these assessments to play a major role in such specific plans as well, but their role here is to inform overall capabilities.

EVALUATING AND TRACKING INDIVIDUAL UTCs

Most of the work in reengineering and reconfiguring specific UTCs will reside with the functional area experts at the MAJCOMs and pilot units. In most cases, tracking UTCs will be diagnostic in purpose, to help identify promising areas of attack for improving the performance at the force/base level.

Evaluation tools can help at this level as well: Previous RAND research on EAF support has used models that can derive specific support capabilities from operational requirements. For example, RAND researchers developed a munitions model that can estimate the equipment and personnel required for the buildup and loading of weapons given operational sortie and mission requirements.[5] RAND also developed a prototype fuel model to simulate transfer and fueling; the model includes personnel, vehicles, pipelines, alternative types of refueling vehicles as well as various forms of fuel storage, and the use of air refueling. Given the operational requirement in terms of sortie rate, the model calculates the manpower and number of refueling trucks of various types required.[6]

These types of models can be used by UTC managers to design and to optimize UTCs and UTC groupings for a given operational capability. They can also make apparent the effect of operational requirements on reducing or increasing certain equipment in the

---

[5]This model was developed by RAND to compute munitions requirement. In its present form, it does not compute the requirement by unit type code but rather by specific munitions or equipment. See Tripp et al., 1999; Amouzegar et al., 2000.

[6]This model is also documented in Tripp et al., 1999.

deployment package. To facilitate the reengineering of UTCs, such models should be developed for many UTCs. In some cases, they will be driven by sortie rates; in other cases, by the number of people deployed; and in still other cases, by a specification of risk and threat to the FOL.

As with force/base packages, the UTCs can also be tracked and, as with the force/base level, this raises the question of which UTCs to track. Clearly one category contains the heaviest UTCs: munitions, civil engineering, Harvest Falcon, and vehicles. However, although these categories would provide the biggest payoff for a given percentage reduction, there may be little scope for reducing deployment requirements other than by prepositioning material in functional areas such as civil engineering and vehicles. The costs and risks must be assessed by the functional areas themselves.

High-technology areas such as medical and communications are also keys for tracking. Current civilian technological advances could have substantial effects on these areas; Unfortunately, these areas are not a major part of the overall footprint.

Some critical support processes are *not* organic to the Air Force at all. These include ground-based air defense ("point defense") and theater missile defense. However, these systems can be heavy and are, by our definition, part of the footprint of an airbase in that they are required in some circumstances to commence and sustain operations. It may therefore be a good idea for the Air Force to track their deployability as well.

EVALUATING AND TRACKING THEATER FOOTPRINT CONFIGURATION

Operational commanders and support planners at the theater level are interested in the deployment and beddown of a large force at multiple sites throughout a theater and in being prepared for several different scenarios. However, with the force/base level understood (including the presence of theater-level facilities such as FSLs), evaluating and tracking the theater-level performance of footprint configurations is then a matter of aggregating the performance at the relevant individual bases.[7]

For tracking strategic improvements in footprint configuration above the theater level, it may be useful to define a set of generic theaters with operational requirements that approximate real theaters but that do not have the specific tailoring associated with the base details of a real theater (how many fire trucks exist at each base, available maintenance facilities, spare housing, etc.). As with force/base packages and individual UTCs, progress at the theater level can be tracked (Table 4.2).

The general procedure suggested here can also be used to track deployment performance in actual theaters as well, of course, and would probably be attractive to individual MAJCOMs. In this case, both strategic support planning and actual warplanning would be working within the same framework and with the same data—a coordination that would make comparisons much easier.

We would expect theater-level tracking to change dynamically with the emergence or reduction of specific threats or conflict situations. Theater infrastructure would probably have a longer lifetime

Table 4.2

Tracking Theater Footprint Configuration (Notional)

| Year | Theater | Scenario | Footprint | | | FSL Footprint | Time (hrs) | | Transportation (C-17 Equiv.) |
			Short Tons	PAX	Short Tons/ Aircraft		IOC	FOC	
2001	Thailand	Near-peer invasion	40,000+	12,103			100	178	509+
2003	Thailand	Near-peer invasion	36,000+	10,356			90	178	

---

[7]If centralized theater support (for repair, supply, RED HORSE teams, etc.) or CONUS support is available, the theater-level model must remove those items from the base lists and determine the appropriate levels at the centralized location or CONUS, accounting for economies of scale and transportation pipelines. The theater-level model should also account for the varying deployment times of units to the theater bases (time-phasing of the footprint configuration).

(although in its planning stage, the techniques suggested here could assess robustness over different scenarios) and may constrain the ability to meet some specific metric goals for new situations. However, the use of a common set of assumptions and data should provide broad confidence in the results at all levels of the footprint hierarchy.

SUMMARY

Much of the Air Force's effort to reduce deployment time and resources has focused on physical footprint reduction, and mainly within individual functional communities. However, although those communities have achieved reductions by policy changes and application of technology, they have also used other strategies such as time-phasing and centralized theater support processes. We argued in the previous chapter that to use all of these strategies in a coherent fashion, the Air Force should use the concept of footprint configuration. However, this more complex concept is multidimensional (in that multiple metrics are needed to describe configurations), and this in turn means that more complex evaluation tools are needed to help decisionmakers choose among configurations. The interaction of support processes and the need to take into account economies of scale for facilities such as FSLs also argue for strong centralized coordination of reconfiguration activities, including evaluation, planning, resource allocation, and tracking. Although there is legitimate interest in the UTC and theater level, the force/base level emerges as the critical focus for evaluating support for expeditionary operations.

Chapter Five

CONCLUSIONS AND RECOMMENDATIONS

The Air Force is committed to the EAF concept and the radical transformation that it requires in the entire Air Force "culture." A central facet of this transformation will be the ability to deploy capable forces quickly to a wide variety of base types. As is evident from the studies cited in Chapter One, there is concern about how quickly even small aerospace forces can deploy to austere locations, at least with current equipment and support processes. Given these concerns and the research reported here, we draw two broad conclusions from our work.

First, although one way to achieve faster deployment is to reduce the raw footprint, this method is only one strategy among many to help speed deployment. The functional areas of the support community have realized that there is more to speeding deployment than simple weight reduction and they are in fact using several different strategies, even when not actually reducing the physical mass of support. What is needed is a framework that includes all the promising strategies so that tradeoffs in deployment time, costs, and risks can be made across strategies and functional areas, allowing selection of a portfolio of strategies that reduce deployment time for *forces*, not individual support processes alone. This has led us to the concept of *footprint configuration* described in Chapter Three.[1]

Second, the focus of footprint (re)configuration efforts for the Air Force should be at what we have termed the force/base level. Al-

---

[1]Similar strategies are being discussed and implemented in other services as well. See, for example, Peltz, Halliday, and Hartman, forthcoming.

though assessment of the feasibility of specific process changes needs to be done at the UTC (or functional level), expecting each functional area to reconfigure itself will likely lead to more of the same problems noted in Chapter Two when simple reduction is the goal: There will be a tendency for each area to try to meet its own goal as best it can, even by getting rid of certain capabilities that still need to be provided by someone else. Since the primary goal is to speed deployment of a force to a base, the effect of any given change must be measured and accepted or rejected on the basis of its performance at this level. Similarly, although strategic decisionmakers at the MAJCOM are primarily interested in the resources required by a theater, the theater is composed of forces deploying to selected bases, so the force/base level is key to the assessment of the theater as well. Even the use of centralized facilities for WRM storage, repair, and transportation needs to be linked to the effects of deploying to individual bases.

We therefore make the following recommendations to act on these conclusions:

Develop a comprehensive, parameterized list of UTCs needed to deploy given force capabilities to different base infrastructures. The input parameters would include the platforms, roles, intensity of flying, base attributes, and aspects such as threat to the FOL for a *generic* force/base. The list would select from a comprehensive list of current UTCs (both reengineered and standard, as desired). This capability is absolutely central to expeditionary planning, even if the Air Force restricts itself to simple footprint reduction, in that it allows the tracking of speed of deployment for a range of forces and destinations. Such a standardized list could provide a starting point for MAJCOM planning, longer-range strategic planning, wargaming, etc. Although it is emphatically not a replacement for deliberate warplans, it should serve to speed the development of those plans and to serve as an objective check on their completeness. Such a list, when operationally tested and trusted,[2] is a central need for an expedi-

_____

[2]We emphasize the need to test these lists to ensure that they are complete and operationally credible, otherwise they will (rightly) be ignored by the planning and operational communities.

tionary force.[3] For the reasons given above, we do not recommend using historical or current TPFDDs directly for this purpose, although they can serve as valuable checks.

Adopt the concept of footprint configuration as an organizing principle for restructuring support processes. As we pointed out in Chapter Two, various functional communities are already using some of the techniques described in Chapter Three. By being able to organize all of the strategies in a common framework with a clear set of metrics, the selection of appropriate strategies for individual support processes will be easier.

Exercise more centralized control of UTC development. Because there is a primary global metric, deployment time, and because different support processes have different masses and reconfiguration options, we believe that more centralization to direct and evaluate efforts is important. Currently, most of the responsibility for making process changes resides at the pilot unit for each UTC. Although the involvement of process experts is key, because the goal is the deployment of a complete force package there needs to be central oversight of the allocation of reengineering effort.[4] The MAJCOM and Air Staff provide some oversight and coordination, but currently no one evaluates the effects of individual proposed changes on force/base package deployments and then allocates resources to those approaches with the biggest payoff at the force/base level. This broad evaluation can be done only above the UTC level and cannot be done by pilot units; it should be the responsibility of MAJCOMs and the Air Staff.

Track changes in deployment speed and other major metrics for selected force packages/base infrastructure combinations to evaluate progress. Given the conclusions and above recommendations, it follows that the way to track progress in footprint reconfiguration is to track the speed of deployment (and other relevant performance metrics) for a selected set of forces and base infrastructures. Some suggestions for the former would be some single-MDS squadrons, the canonical 36-ship ASETF, the current "pop-up" forces led by the

---

[3]It is telling that Air Staff studies on the feasibility of ASETF deployment have generated such a list several times from scratch.

[4]Hess and Wermund, 1992.

366th and the 4th Fighter Wing, and perhaps some single-MDS six-ship packages. For base infrastructures, it seems advisable to use at least a generic international airport and bare base.

It has been suggested that it would be instructive to evaluate the improvement in footprint since the inception of the EAF concept in the mid-1990s. As noted above, the lack of a set of parameterized UTC lists is a major obstacle. Moreover, from the partial analyses of Chapter Two, it seems clear that severe data problems would require extensive work to overcome, particularly in establishing the "baseline" footprint. Further, it seems likely that there has been a slight overall increase, primarily because of changes in requirements (e.g., fire risk), even as some specific areas have at least reduced the mass of IOR.

Set up a system to aggregate the force/base evaluations to theater level for current warplans and for strategic support planning for proposed plans. As with the force/base evaluations, this would track changes in deployment speed, time to IOC, and deployment resources, but now for a theaterwide plan for basing and employing expeditionary forces. However, other metrics would also be important at this level, including permanent infrastructure expenditures and assessments of availability and vulnerability of the infrastructure. In the current defense structure, these evaluations are clearly of interest to the MAJCOMs supporting the several geographic combatant commanders, and each would probably wish to set up its own tracking system using actual theater plans. But recent events such as the operations in Kosovo and Afghanistan have indicated that many major operations will draw operational forces and support from several combatant commanders and so a corporate tracking system to evaluate all warplans for review as a whole by senior Air Force leadership may be an emerging necessity. As with coordinating UTC development centrally, this will be a move toward more centralized overview of a support system that is increasingly seen in global terms.[5]

Develop tools to help decisionmakers evaluate and select among alternative footprint configurations. We presented some prototype

---

[5]Tripp et al., 1999.

tools in Chapter Four that use data at the UTC level and, depending on some selections of footprint configuration, evaluate some of the metrics proposed in Chapter Three. Such a tool (together with the parameterized UTC lists advocated above) would allow analysts to evaluate quickly many different footprint configurations rigorously. Because we do not expect there to be a configuration that dominates in all metrics simultaneously, decisionmakers will also need tools to organize the results of evaluating different configurations to allow them to weight the results of individual metrics and come to a final decision. This is in line with the view that logistics must become a *strategic* planning function in an expeditionary world.[6]

---

[6]Tripp et al., 2000.

Amouzegar, Mahyar, Lionel Galway, and Amanda Geller, *Supporting Expeditionary Aerospace Forces: Alternatives for Jet Engine Intermediate Maintenance*, Santa Monica, Calif.: RAND, MR-1431-AF, 2001.

Amouzegar, Mahyar, Lionel Galway, and Robert S. Tripp, "Production and Management of Munitions for the Expeditionary Air Force," *WDSI 2000 Proceedings*, Western Decision Science Institute, Twenty-Ninth Annual Meeting, Hawaii, April 18–22, 2000, pp. 935–942.

Feinberg, Amatzia, Hyman L. Shulman, Louis W. Miller, and Robert S. Tripp, *Supporting Expeditionary Aerospace Forces: Expanded Analysis of LANTIRN Options*, Santa Monica, Calif.: RAND, MR-1225-AF, 2001a.

Feinberg, Amatzia, Robert S. Tripp, James Leftwich, Eric Peltz, Mahyar A. Amouzegar, Russell Grunch, John Drew, and Charles R. Roll, *Supporting Expeditionary Aerospace Forces: Lessons from the Air War Over Serbia*, Santa Monica, Calif.: RAND, MR-1263-AF, 2001b. [Restricted, For Official Use Only]

Galway, Lionel A., Robert S. Tripp, Timothy L. Ramey, and CMSgt John G. Drew, *Supporting Expeditionary Aerospace Forces: New Agile Combat Support Postures*, Santa Monica, Calif.: RAND, MR-1075-AF, 2000.

Hagel, Stephen J., "Capturing Logistics Data, Part II," *Air Force Journal of Logistics*, Vol. 16, Winter 1992.

Hess, Jeffrey M., and Merry D. Wermund, *Analysis of Standard Type Unit Development*, master's thesis, Air Force Institute of Technology, AFIT/GLM/LSM/92S-23, Wright-Patterson AFB, Ohio, 1992.

Hillestad, Richard J., and Paul K. Davis, *Resource Allocation for the New Defense Strategy: The DynaRank Decision-Support System*, Santa Monica, Calif.: RAND, MR-996-OSD, 1998.

Killingsworth, Paul, Lionel A. Galway, Eiichi Kamiya, Brian Nichiporuk, Timothy L. Ramey, Robert S. Tripp, and James C. Wendt, *Flexbasing: Achieving Global Presence for Expeditionary Aerospace Forces*, Santa Monica, Calif.: RAND, MR-1113-AF, 2000.

O'Fearna, Frank C., *Reduction of the Aircraft Ground Equipment: Footprint of an Air Expeditionary Force*, master's thesis, Air Force Institute of Technology, AFIT/GOR/ENS/99M-14, Wright-Patterson AFB, Ohio, March 1999.

Peltz, Eric, John Halliday, and Steven Hartman, "Combat Service Support Transformation: Emerging Strategies for Making the Power Projection Army a Reality," Santa Monica, Calif.: RAND, forthcoming.

Peltz, Eric, Hyman L. Shulman, Robert S. Tripp, Timothy Ramey, Randy King, and John G. Drew, *Supporting Expeditionary Aerospace Forces: An Analysis of F-15 Avionics Options*, Santa Monica, Calif.: RAND, MR-1174-AF, 2000.

Ryan, General Michael E., *Evolving to an Expeditionary Aerospace Force*, Commander's NOTAM 98-4, Washington, D.C., July 28, 1998.

Sweetman, Bill, "Expeditionary USAF sets course," *Jane's International Defense Review*, Vol. 33, May 2000.

Synergy, Inc., "Bare Base Analysis," briefing, January 12, 1999.

Tripp, Robert S., Lionel A. Galway, Timothy L. Ramey, Mahyar Amouzegar, and Eric L. Peltz, *Supporting Expeditionary Aerospace Forces: A Concept for Evolving to the Agile Combat Support/ Mobility System of the Future*, Santa Monica, Calif.: RAND, MR-1179-AF, 2000.

Tripp, Robert S., Lionel A. Galway, Paul S. Killingsworth, Eric L. Peltz, Timothy L. Ramey, and John G. Drew, *Supporting Expeditionary Aerospace Forces: An Integrated Strategic Agile Combat Support Planning Framework*, Santa Monica, Calif.: RAND, MR-1056-AF, 1999.

U.S. Air Force, *Air Force Vision 2020: Global Vigilance, Reach and Power*, Washington D.C., 2001.

U.S. Air Force, "Civil Engineer Expeditionary Combat Support," briefing, AF/ILE, July 24, 2000.

U.S. Air Force, *Operations Plan and Concept Plan Development and Implementation*, Air Force Manual 10-401, Washington D.C., 1999.

U.S. Air Force, *Guide to Bare Base Development*, Vol. 1, Air Force Handbook 10-222, Washington, D.C., July 1, 1996.

U.S. Air Force, "United States Air Force UTC Refinement Effort," briefing, AF/XOXW, n.d.

Vo, Tam T., *Exploratory Analysis of the Deployment Feasibility of United States Air Force Air Expeditionary Forces*, Air Force Institute of Technology, Wright-Patterson AFB, Ohio, September 1997.